"Dear Mam..."

Letters and Memories of a
Liverpool Soldier in Vietnam
1966-67

By

Derek Ponting

To Joe & Cathy.

Hope you enjoy the book!.
Happy Xmas
Dec 2011

Best Wishes Degsy

First Published 2011 by Countyvise Ltd
14 Appin Road, Birkenhead, CH41 9HH

British Library Cataloguing in Publication Data.
A catalogue record for this book is available from the British Library.

ISBN 978 1 906823 58 0

Dedication

This book is dedicated to the memory of all those Australians who died as a result of the Vietnam War.

To my Army pal the late Don Castagna.

In Loving Memory of my dear Mam.

Acknowledgments

I'd like to thank Peter Guy a colleague I worked with on the buses. Peter helped me to arrange the format of the book and also gave me the book's title.

Many thanks also to my old Army mates who supplied me with photos and forgotten memories.

And last but not least I'd like to thank my wife Pat for typing up this book from my handwritten notes.

Introduction

When I emigrated to Australia on 14th February 1965 as a 19-year-old (six weeks before my 20th birthday) I was totally unaware of Australia's involvement in the Vietnam War.

I also had no idea that Australia had introduced National Service for 20 year olds, which also applied to British subjects entering the country.

When I arrived in Australia it came as quite a shock to be told there was a possibility I could be drafted into the Armed Forces.

My first thought was "why wasn't I told about this when I attended the interview back in the UK? Would I still have emigrated had I known about it beforehand?" I'm not really sure. However, fate played its hand and I was called up on 29th September 1965. I served two years National Service and did a tour of duty in Vietnam.

Looking back I don't have any regrets because my experiences made me realise how fortunate I've been. The friends and comradeship I made in Australia and Vietnam have been invaluable to me.

This is my story of how the events that took place between February 1965 and December 1967 changed my life forever.

Derek Ponting

Diary of events

1964: November 10, the Australian Government introduces the Barrel Lottery conscription for two years National Service for 20 year olds.

1965: April 29· the Australian Government announces that combat troops will go into Vietnam. The first battalion leaves in June.

1966: The first conscripts are sent to Vietnam. May 24 first conscript dies in Vietnam

1966: August 18, The Battle of Long Tan claims the lives of 18 Australian Soldiers. August 18 chosen to be Australia's Vietnam Veterans Day, in memory of the fallen soldiers.

1975: April 25, Australia completes its withdrawal from Vietnam, Anzac Day.

In all 50,000 Australian Troops went to Vietnam. 500 died (200 conscripts) and 2,400 were wounded.

Many more returned home emotionally scarred.

Contents

CHAPTER ONE

LIVERPOOL TO MELBOURNE

I remember it was a bitterly cold morning one day in November 1964. I was standing at the bus stop waiting for the bus to take me to work. I always hated the cold weather (and still do) and I wondered if one day I could get a job somewhere in another country with a warm climate.

Then a few days later I thought all my prayers had been answered, when I read an advert in the Liverpool Echo. Railway staff were wanted to work in Australia. Victoria Railways in Melbourne wanted Station Assistants and Trainee Shunters. I thought "this is my chance to get away from this cold weather at last!"

My Cousin Les lived in Maghull and I knew he would be interested in the jobs, so I phoned him and told him about the advert in the Echo.

Interviews were being held in Liverpool City Centre, so me and Les decided to go along and see what it was all about. We decided to give it a go and we applied, filling in numerous application forms we then had a medical examination.

Weeks later we were told we had been accepted and we would be given a date to leave for Australia in the near future.

We were really looking forward to making the journey together but we were given different dates! My date was 14th February 1965 and Les left two weeks before me.

The Australian Government, under the Assisted Passage Scheme paid for our flights. The only money we had to pay was £10 each. That's why the Aussies called us "£10 Poms". If you returned home within two years, you had to pay back the full fare.

About a month before I was due to leave for Australia, I got the impression that my Mother thought I wouldn't go. I'm sure she thought I would back out at the last minute, but as the time drew closer and Les had already left for Australia, she finally accepted that I was going to leave. Money was a bit of an issue at the time, although I had a job to go to and my accommodation was also sorted out at the Railway hostel in Melbourne, but I hardly had any money. My Mother and Father didn't have any savings, but they gave me what they could and I remember I also got a few bob from my Mother's sister Auntie Peg.

Altogether I had a grand total of £17 10s about £17.50, not a lot when you are starting a new life on the other side of the world. However, my hopes were raised for a bit more cash the day before I was due to leave. My Mother told me that Pop McEvitt wanted to see me, and she thought he would give me some money to see me on my way, after all I had known him since I was a kid! Pop was in his 70s and he owned the greengrocers a few doors away from our house, everyone thought he was a wealthy man. I had heard that at one time he used to live in Australia so I was hoping he would give me some advice too. Off I went to see him and as I really expected I never got any money off him, however, he did give me some advice which at the time I thought was very funny, he told me to always wear a vest! I thought to myself am I hearing this right. I'm going to Australia to get away from the cold weather and he's telling me to keep a vest on! When I got back home and told my Mother we both fell about laughing.

When it came to the time for me to leave and say my goodbyes my Mother seemed quite calm at first until I said "Well Mam I'll have to go now," she threw her arms around me and broke down. She knew then it would be at least two years before she would see me again. I gave my Father and my brother Brian a hug, kissed Lassie our dog and then I was off to Lime Street station to catch the train to London. When I arrived at the airport, I checked in for the flight to Melbourne, my luggage consisted of one small holdall. I had painted the words Melbourne Australia on both sides of the bag to make it easier to recognise. The bag contained a few shirts, a couple of pairs of trousers, some underwear, one pair of shoes, some toiletries and that was about it! I put the holdall on the scales and the check-in girl asked me did I have any more luggage? "No" I replied. "Do you have any hand luggage?" Again "No" I replied, with a puzzled look on her face she said so this small bag is the only thing you're taking to Australia with you? That's correct I said, looking back I can see why she was surprised, after all the journey from London to Melbourne in 1965 took about 38 hrs! The planes then had propellers not jet engines like they are today, and we stopped to refuel five times. Some of the places we stopped at were Beirut, Tehran, New Delhi, Singapore, Darwin and finally Melbourne! With no hand luggage for the whole trip I hadn't had a shave since the morning I left home. Fortunately I have never had a thick growth, but after about 48 hours without a shave I looked like Worzul Gummage! I don't know what kind of an impression I gave the guy from the Railways who came to pick me up at the airport, but I can guess that it wasn't a good one.

He was supposed to pick me and another bloke up, but the other person didn't show up so we set off in his car to the Railway Hostel. When I left England the temperature was just above freezing, when I arrived in Australia it was 90 degrees and it was early morning. We drove through Melbourne, passed the MCG which is a very impressive stadium. As we entered the city centre, I noticed all the businessmen going to work with their briefcases in hand. However, there were no suits on view! They wore shirt and tie, shorts and knee high socks, and surprise surprise, they were all wearing vests under their shirts! I was told this was to help with perspiration so Pop McEvitt's advice wasn't so daft after all.

When we arrived at the hostel, I was put in the same room as my cousin Les. He was out at work so I began to unpack. It wasn't long before I heard a shout from the corridor 'Scouse, Scouse!' I opened the door and there was this bloke who said "are you a Scouser?" "yes" I said "so am I" he said - "everyone calls me Ginge," I thought

I've just come 12,000 miles and one of the first people I meet is a Scouser, small world or what! Ginge was also a £10 Pom and had been working on the railways for about six months.

We got talking and when I told him how old I was he said did I know that I had to register for National Service. I thought he must be mistaken, but I thought I had better check so a few days later I went to the Army recruiting office to find out. I told them I had just arrived from the UK and that I would be 20 years old next month. I was told that I had to register - all 20 years old from the UK had to register he said. "What happens if I don't register" I said, "If you do that and the authorities catch up with you, you'll be fined £50 and called-up anyway" he said. But the words he used that stuck in my mind more than anything else was "Don't worry though, it's a million to one chance you'll get called up anyway, because they are only picking a few birth dates out so you'll be unlucky if one of them is yours!" Well, you don't have to be Albert Einstein to work out that there are 365 days in a year, which cuts the odds down quite a bit from a million to one! Regardless of the odds I had to register. My cousin Les was three years older than me and was exempt from registering.

In one of my first letters to my Mother I explained what had gone on and mentioned the million to one chance, so she must have been very convinced that I wouldn't be called up.

I found out at a much later date that in the first national service ballot, 96 birth dates were drawn between 1st Jan 1965 and 30th June 1965, which made the odds of being called up about 50-50! So it was no surprise really that my birth date the 28th March was picked out.

CHAPTER TWO

MELBOURNE TO ADELAIDE

After a couple of days settling in it was time to start my new job. Originally I was going to be a Station Assistant, because you had to be 21 years old to be a Trainee Shunter, but when I got there they had lowered the age limit so I decided to take the Trainee Shunter job instead the same as Les. But looking back I think that was my first mistake, because of what followed.

My first day on the job I was taken to the clothing store to be kitted out. I was given a blue boiler suit and a blue hat. I laughed when I saw the hat, because it was the same type that Hopalong Cassidy or Hoss Cartwright would wear. I think it was called a ten-gallon hat. So, I put the hat and the boiler suit on and I was ready for my first day's work. However, the foreman thought observation was the order of the day. He said "All I want you to do is sit on that bench, watch what goes on and take in as much as you can." So that's what I did all day - with my big hat and boiler suit on I sat and watched the trains going backwards and forwards, with the sweat pouring off me. It must have been 90 degrees, I never thought that after just a few days in Australia I'd be hoping for cooler weather, when all the time in England I had been complaining about the cold! Anyway, I thought tomorrow I'll probably be jumping on and off trains and getting a bit of a breeze. The next morning the foreman said to me "Did you observe what went on yesterday?" "Yes," I replied, "That's good" he said, "I want you to do the same again today, just take in what you can" I thought, I haven't come 12000 miles to sit on a bench watching trains going up and down! By lunchtime I was really pissed off and decided I'd had enough, so I got up off the bench and headed back to the hostel. When Les got in from his shift I told him what had happened and I said I wasn't going back, "what are we going to do now" he said. I said "I had heard about the grape picking season starting in Adelaide, South Australia and that I wouldn't mind giving that a go. So Les said he would pack the job in too and come with me. The next day we gave in our notice at the railway, and as you can imagine they were furious with us and told us so in no uncertain terms! They said we were ungrateful and hadn't really given the job a chance, which to be fair was right.

However, we had made up our minds and that was it! They said we would be put out of the hostel the next day, which I suppose was understandable. We went back to the hostel and packed our gear ready to be off the next day. The day was still really hot so we decided to make the most of our last day in Melbourne and headed off to the nearby swimming pool. That turned out to be one big mistake! It was an outdoor pool and when we arrived there we were two shades lighter than a bottle of milk, but within a couple of hours we were the colour of over ripe tomatoes! We'd committed the cardinal sin of not using any sun cream and we were about to pay the price. It was too late when we realised what had happened that we'd well and truly over done it. On the way back to the hostel we stopped off at a pub for a few drinks. When we were just about to leave I noticed that Les had this vacant look on his face! The next thing I knew he had collapsed on the floor, he was suffering from sun stroke and was semi-conscious. After a couple of minutes he came round and we got a taxi back to the hostel. We were both badly burned and in a lot of pain, but Les was a lot worse than me. He had blisters all over him and his feet swelled up like balloons. My shoulders were blistered and I was burning all over. We had to be out of the hostel the next day and I wondered how we were going to cope on the long train journey to Adelaide. Somehow we managed it, but it was so uncomfortable we didn't catch a wink of sleep. When we finally arrived in Adelaide Les's feet were even more swollen and he could hardly walk. He was shuffling along and he must have been in a lot of pain. But watching him I couldn't help seeing the funny side of things, because he looked like he'd shit himself and I just couldn't stop laughing. Of course Les didn't see the funny side and I'm sure he would have punched me if he had been able to!

Because of our sunburn, we couldn't start work picking grapes in the scorching heat. Fortunately, Les knew a family who lived in Para Hills, a suburb of Adelaide. He got in touch with them and they said they would put us up for a few days.

Once we had recovered from the sunburn we had to find a job. We had run out of money as we had spent what little we had on taxi and train fares. The family we were staying with kindly lent us some money and said we could pay them back when we started working. So without their help and generosity I don't know how or where we would have ended up.

CHAPTER THREE

GRAPE PICKING IN RENMARK

We found out that grape pickers were needed in Renmark, a small town about 160 miles north of Adelaide, so we headed off up there. Once we arrived in Renmark we more or less got fixed up with jobs straight away. A man who owned a local vineyard came into town to pick us up. His name was Mr Guscott. He told us that we'd need to buy some Tucker (Food) as we'd have to do our own cooking something we weren't expecting. "You'll also have to buy some hats" he said. We didn't have much money left so we said we wouldn't bother with hats, he said that if we didn't wear hats he wouldn't be able to employ us, you won't last one day in this heat he said, so we took his advice and bought a couple of cheap straw hats and some food to last us until the weekend.

He drove us to his vineyard which was about 2 miles away and told us the grape picking season would last about 10 - 12 weeks. We intended to stay until the season finished so I decided to inform the Army authorities of my new address, this was one of the conditions that I had to comply with.

As we approached the vineyard, Mr Guscott pointed to his house which was a big detached place in its own grounds. A bit further on we came to our house - I'm not sure what I was expecting but it came as a bit of a shock! At first I thought it was some sort of animal shed, it was made of tin and I couldn't see any windows. However, when I got closer, I could see a small window next to the door and when we got inside it looked a lot better than the outside! It had two single beds, a small table and a couple of chairs, a cooker, cabinet and pots, pans and cutlery, and thank goodness the essential shower. The only snag was there was no hot water so it was a cold shower every night, but that wasn't a problem because it was so hot. In fact it was more than 100 degrees every day for the first week and after that it never fell below 90 degrees F. Despite the heat Les always kept long sleeves shirts, long trousers and a hat on. He was making sure he wasn't going to get burnt again like he did in Melbourne.

I was a bit more adventurous, I often took my shirt off for a couple of hours each day and I ended up with a good tan! However, one day I didn't heed Mr Guscott's advice and I decided to leave my hat off and I paid the price! The next day my face was badly burnt and of course my nose got the worse of it. It broke out in blisters and swelled up so much it looked like a blind cobbler's thumb, but I was warned so I had only myself to blame!

Anyway after we had been shown our accommodation, Mr Guscott explained he needed only one of us to pick grapes and the other one to help him load the crates of grapes onto the tractor, the grapes would then be unloaded onto racks and dried in the sun to become sultanas.

We agreed that I'd help the boss as you had to drive the tractor and Les couldn't drive. We were to start work the following morning. As it was only midday we asked the boss if there was anywhere nearby where we could have a swim as it was so hot and we really needed to cool off. The boss pointed to a dirt track and told us to follow it for about half a mile and we would come to a creek, just watch out for snakes on your way down to it, he said. Me and Les looked at each other as though to say let's give it a miss, but on second thoughts it was so hot we decided to go, we had only gone about a hundred yards when we came to sudden halt..... Right across the path in front of us was an army of marching ants! They weren't small ants that you would get back home, they were Bull ants and apparently they had one hell of a bite, so you could imagine how painful it would be if a few hundred crawled up your leg and bit you! I remember someone telling me if you stood on them you wouldn't crush them, they'd carry on walking! I know that was an exaggeration but you would still be wise to give them a wide birth. Anyway we decided to carry on, so we took a run up and jumped over them. When we reached the creek I was really disappointed, I expected to see nice clear water, and instead it was a dirty rust colour and didn't look at all inviting! However, I thought I've come this far, braved bull ants, risked possible snake bites.... the sweat's pouring off me so I'm going in! From the bank you couldn't tell how deep it was and Les couldn't swim so we looked for a spot where we could paddle, as we looked around we saw a small rowing boat tied up along the bank, there wasn't a soul around so we jumped into it and Les rowed out into the middle of the creek. I was still reluctant to go in because of how murky it looked and I wondered what was beneath the water. I thought it must be safe otherwise the boss would have told us, so after plucking up the courage I dived in! The water was warm but it still cooled me down as I swam around. Les stayed in the boat and I noticed he was starting to drift away from me and I could see he was heading for something sticking out of the water! Then I realised what it was - it was the carcass of a large dead animal - I think it was a cow. I shouted out to warn Les but it was too late and he bumped right into it. He got such a fright and he began to row as fast as he could back to me - he had me laughing my head off again. I quickly got out and needless to say we never went back to that creek again. In fact we never strayed far from our hut even when we had a bit of spare time on our hands, because we were living right by a swamp. It was really scary at night with lots of strange noises going on outside the hut, especially for two Poms who are not used to wild animals running around outside their house. At night it was pitch black and as there was no toilet in the hut we had to use an outside toilet that was about 10 yards away. You had to take a torch with you when you needed to go! If we wanted a pee, we would use the shower rather than risk going outside in the pitch black. I recall one particular night when I really needed to go for a No 2 and I couldn't wait until morning. The toilet was in a small shed and of course there was no flush (something I would get used to in Vietnam). Torch in hand I set off and got to the toilet and sat down, after a couple of minutes I heard a rustling sound coming from underneath the door, I shined the torch down and saw a forked tongue! Straight away I thought it was a snake but then the head appeared and I could see it was a lizard, but I still shit myself, thankfully I was in the right place!

After a hard day's work we were always tired, so we never had any trouble getting off to sleep, except the noises would often wake us up. We mentioned this to the boss and he said he would bring us a mains radio so that we could play some music to help distract us from the noises and it did the trick.

We had to do all our own cooking and that was a first for both of us. I'm ashamed to say I don't think I had even boiled an egg back home, my Mother used to cook all my meals and do all my washing and ironing. Now it was our turn to get domesticated.

Every Saturday morning Les and I would hitchhike into Renmark to do our week's shopping. Every week we bought the same things, bread, soup, eggs, bacon, beans and biscuits, which as you can imagine our meals were the same nearly every day. We didn't bother with breakfast, but lunch was a bowl of soup with half a dozen slices of bread and dinner was eggs, bacon and beans on toast, and for supper coffee and biscuits. We never varied it and believe it or not we never got fed up of eating the same things for the whole time we were there. Perhaps it had something to do with working so hard out in the open as we were always hungry.

One week things went a bit differently.... this particular Saturday the boss asked if we would like to work, we said ok and he told us to write our grocery list and his wife would get the weekly shop for us. Not a problem I thought. After we finished work we went back to the hut and all our groceries were inside on the table, but we got a shock when we saw that the 14 tins of beans we asked for were 14 tins of sliced green beans, so it was no baked beans for one week! The only consolation was the air in the hut smelt a lot sweeter, if you know what I mean!

One day we got a surprise when Mrs Guscott came round to our hut and invited us to have Sunday lunch "Do you like roast lamb?" she asked! "Er yes" we said - it was music to our ears. So when Sunday came around we got cleaned up and headed over to the house and had our first proper meal since we had left home, we thought all our birthdays had come at once.

As the grape picking season was coming to an end I think we had spent about 10 weeks at the vineyard altogether, and during that time I had a few mishaps! I recall the time I reversed the tractor into the grape vine and knocked a post over. Another time I nearly wrecked the grape dip when I accidentally let go of the winching handle but I just managed in the nick of time to put the ratchet brake on before it smashed into it, the spinning handle caught me below the shoulder and caused a deep gash.

I also managed to fall off the back of the trailer a few times! All in all I really enjoyed the time I spent working for Mr Guscott. I remember his teenage daughter Judy too. I recall one night Judy asked me and Les if we would like to go into town with her to watch a movie. We had previously only been into town on Saturday mornings to do our weekly shopping, so we took her up on the offer. We thought it would be a nice change from being cooped up in our stifling hot tin shed to sitting in a nice air conditioned cinema. However, we were a bit surprised when we got there. It was certainly air conditioned alright, but not in the way that we expected, by that, I mean it was an open-air cinema and instead of the usual cinema seats everyone was sitting in deckchairs! Anyway, it made a nice change watching a movie under the stars. Me and Judy exchanged a few letters when I was in Vietnam. I can't remember why we didn't carry on writing, but I suspect that it was probably my doing, and if it was I apologise and hope after all this time she has forgiven me.

With the grape picking season finally over Les and I had to decide what to do next. We considered a few things like Opal mining, Gold prospecting and Sugar Cane cutting. Mr Guscott told us that sugar cane cutting was back breaking work but the pay was very good, so we decided to give that a go. The only trouble was we had to travel to North Queensland which was a few thousand miles away, but the good thing was we were following the warm weather as well. Mr

Guscott told us to go to Mackay, a town about 500 miles north of Brisbane. He said the sugar cane cutting season would be starting soon.

When I left Renmark I hadn't heard from the Army and I thought well no news is good news.

*Me and Les outside
our living quarters.
(Renmark
South Australia)*

Me and Les ready to start work. (Renmark South Australia)

Me unloading the crates of grapes onto the racks so they can be dried into sultanas. (Renmark South Australia)

Me and Les doing early morning exercise with heavy tractor axel. (Renmark South Australia)

Me and Les with Mr and Mrs Guscott at their house.

They invited us around for Sunday lunch. (Renmark South Australia)

Me and Les with Mrs Guscott on the Murray River. (Renmark South Australia)

Me and Les having a day off on the Murray River. (Renmark South Australia)

CHAPTER FOUR

ON THE ROAD AGAIN!

So, me and Les were on our travels again and our first stop was Para Hills to pay back the money we had borrowed and to thank the family once again for their kindness.

We then boarded the train in Adelaide and headed back to Melbourne. Once we arrived there we decided to look up some of the guys we had met at the Railway hostel. As it happened someone had organised a party for that night and we got invited and had a really good time. The next day we suffered with terrible hangovers, which was not surprising because we hadn't had a drop of alcohol all the time we had been in South Australia.

The next day we arranged the second part of our trip, which was a train journey to Sydney, by this time we were getting used to long train journeys and to be honest we enjoyed them, because you could stretch out, have a walk up and down and we saw some fantastic scenery along the way.

When we arrived in Sydney we booked into the YMCA and then went sightseeing. One of the first places on the agenda was the Sydney Harbour Bridge. Me and Les went up one of the towers and had our lunch overlooking the Opera House. At that time it was still being built, but it was still a magnificent sight.

That night we went to Kings Cross where all the entertainment is. We had a great night in the bars and clubs, but it was a lot more expensive than we thought it would be and we spent more than we should have done, but it was worth it.

The following day we were on the move again, back on another train heading for Brisbane and more sightseeing. As our money was getting a bit short we said we had to start taking things a bit easier. We didn't have a bank account and all our wages in Renmark were paid in cash, so we always had to carry all our money with us. I had some of it in my wallet and Les carried most of it round his waist in a money belt.

One morning he woke up and the money belt was gone! We looked all over the room and couldn't find it, we were devastated and couldn't think what had happened. We went into the bathroom and there it was in the bath! Les must have taken it off the night before when he was pissed, we were so relieved but it didn't half give us a scare. We still had quite a bit further to go up North before we reached the Sugar cane areas. We left Brisbane and headed north, once again by train. We went through Bundaberg, Gladstone and Rockhampton before we eventually reached our destination in Mackay. We were hoping to get fixed up straight away with jobs cutting the sugar cane but to our surprise and shock we found out the cane cutting season had already started and all the jobs had been filled.

We had travelled 3000 miles and with our money nearly all gone, and then to be told there were no jobs at the end you can imagine how we felt. We were absolutely gutted and thought what the hell are we going to do now!

The first thing we had to do was to find somewhere to stay and get something to eat. We found a small boarding house which was quite cheap and they let you pay on a daily basis, and you could also pay for your meals as you went along.

A few days went past and we tried everything but still no sign of any work. We were virtually skint and we were getting desperate. We were strolling around town wondering what we would do next as we had practically given up on finding a job. We stopped outside an office building and Les said let's ask in here if anyone knows about

25

any jobs going. I thought it was a waste of time but we had nothing to lose so we walked in. There were people working at their desks. I went up to one girl and asked her if she knew of any jobs going anywhere. I'm sorry she said there's nothing going around here, our hearts sank again and we were about to leave when she said, we have vacancies for two bridge labourers if you are prepared to work out in the bush. We immediately said we would do it and she said we could start work the next day, we couldn't believe our luck, we were made up.

First we had to travel by train to St Lawrence but it wasn't an ordinary train it was a freight train, which meant that there was only one carriage for passengers and that was at the rear.

In the passenger compartment with me and Les there was a woman passenger. She looked like she was in her 60s but she was probably only about 40... she looked really rough and she was obviously an alcoholic as she had a large bottle of vodka in her hand and she was pissed out of her head. She was wearing a long white dress or should I say off-white and it looked like someone's wedding dress from the 1930s. The carriage consisted of two long seats opposite one another and you couldn't access any other part of the train, I think it was originally meant for the crew and not only that there were two empty spaces were the doors should have - not too hot on health and safety in those days! After we had been travelling for a while I noticed that the woman's Vodka bottle was nearly empty. The next think I knew she got up from her seat and she mumbled something about needing a pee, the train was doing about 30 mph and there was no way that she could get off or out of the carriage so she just lifted up her dress and squatted down, stuck her arse out of the door space and relieved herself. Me and Les looked at each other and burst out laughing!

When we finally arrived at St Lawrence, it was about three in the morning and there wasn't a soul around at the station. We approached the train driver who was getting out of his cab and told him we were supposed to meet someone here about a job. He said whoever it is would probably be staying at the pub and pointed us towards the town. We headed off passing a butchers shop, a post office and a few houses and that was it! A typical Aussie bush town. As we got near the pub there was no one around and it was in darkness. It had swing doors, the type you see in saloons in the cowboy movies, so we just walked in, and the place was empty. We decided to get some kip so we pulled a few chairs up and stretched out. Just as I was about to drop off I heard a noise behind me and I felt my chair move, I opened my eyes and got the fright of my life as I stared down the barrel of a shotgun, a voice said "what the fuck d'you think you're doing? It was the pub Landlord. After we got over the initial shock, we told him we were supposed to meet someone about a job. He realised we were genuine and gave us a room for the rest of the night, but if I'd had my way I'd have stayed where I was because there was only a couple of hours until daybreak and we could have saved the money he charged us for the room! However, you don't argue with someone holding a gun! Later that morning when we got up he said he was sorry for putting the shits up us, he said he had the gun for any wild animals that might wander in.

The guy we were supposed to meet turned up a bit later and introduced himself as Jim. He was the foreman in charge of the bridge labourers. After we got acquainted, I asked him for the address where we would be staying so that I could inform the Army, and he gave me a PO Box No in St Lawrence and said the mail was picked up every weekend and brought to us in the bush.

He said our camp was about a 2 hour drive through the bush. Before we left, he told us we had to buy a week's rations, but we told him we didn't have any money, we'd just given our last few bob to the pub landlord! So he lent us the money and it was to be taken back from our first week's wages. Once gain we had to do our own cooking, but at least this time we were a bit more experienced. We still got our usual tins of beans but we also got some meat from the butchers. We loaded everything into Jim's truck and set off along the dirt road through the bush to our camp. When we arrived, we met three other guys who we would be working with. One was from Sweden, I think he was in his 50s and the other two guys were from Sarina which was a town about 20 miles away. They were only young about 16 years old, but one of them was built like a brick shithouse and about 6 feet tall and weighed about 15 stone. When he told me his name I couldn't help but laugh to myself ....he was called Vivian! I thought he's got to be joking! But he wasn't. I remember a few years later when I heard that Johnny Cash song about a Boy named Sue and it reminded me of Vivian! I wondered if he had the same problem with his name, especially with him looking so macho! Another thing that I remember about him was that he never wore anything on his feet! He used to walk around the camp barefoot, and I noticed the soles of his feet were like leather. He told me that when he was a kid he always went around without any shoes on. I remember he turned out to be a nice friendly guy.

The other young lad was friendly as well, although once due to a misunderstanding he got annoyed with me. Without wanting to sound too insulting to him, I think he was a bit slow, or a bit limp under the cap, if you know what I mean! I hadn't mixed with many Aussies up to that point so I wasn't too familiar with their slang words and sayings. It wasn't until I'd been working with them for a while that I picked up some of them, such as "fair dinkum", "she's right mate", "G'day" and "How ya goin", but this young lads favourite saying was "my bloody oath", however, he pronounced oath as oaf due to his slight speech impediment. With me not being familiar with the term, I asked him what oaf meant! He must have thought that I was taking the piss because he got really angry saying "Oaf, it's what you do when you swear on the bible!" that's when the penny finally dropped. But we still got on well together after that.

In the camp there were small box shaped portable cabins, inside there were two single beds with mattresses and that was it, no blankets. At first we thought that wouldn't be a problem, after all we were in sunny Queensland! But we didn't know how cold it got at night. In fact it was so cold that first night we pushed the two beds together and covered ourselves with an old tarpaulin that we got from the back of the truck. We ended up a bit squashed but it served the purpose.

Keeping warm in the hut wasn't our only problem, we had to keep a look out for Red Back spiders as they used to nest in the corners of the hut and underneath the beds. The foreman had told us if you ever get bitten by one they'll make you that crook (ill) you'll be in bed for days, so he put the shits up us from the start! He told us to avoid being bitten we should light a piece of paper and before we get into bed, burn around the corners of the hut, we did this for about a week when we realised no one else was doing it, they were all having a right old laugh at the stupid Poms! The Red Back spider was poisonous and would give you a nasty bite but if left alone it wouldn't harm you. In fact one of them ran right across the back of my hand when I was straightening a calendar in the hut and fortunately it didn't bite me!

All the cooking and eating was done out in the open.

Anyway the job we were here to do was to build a small bridge over a gully that used to flood in the wet season and vehicles weren't able to get across. We also had to repair some of the other wooden bridges in the area as well. Termites used to eat inside the wooden pylons that supported the bridges to such an extent that some were practically hollow. We used to pour this yellow poison inside them and the termites seemed to thrive on it. I used to wonder how these pylons managed to stay up. The one we were working on was going to have concrete supports to last a lot longer. The weather was very pleasant to work in during the day, it was usually in the high 60s. I used to work in a pair of shorts so I could keep my tan, Les of course as usual kept covered up! I had never worked as a labourer before so I wasn't familiar with some of the tools we used. I remember when the foreman asked me to pass him the mattock, I didn't have a clue what he wanted, so not to show my ignorance I said "has anyone seen the mattock?" One of the lads pointed in the direction of a spade and what looked like a pickaxe, except it was flat at one end. I knew what a spade was so it had to be other one, which it was.

On my day off I would sometimes stroll on my own and walk for miles around the bush. I used to watch the wild kangaroos hopping around as well as all the other wild animals. It was a completely different world to what I was used to back at home in Liverpool and perhaps that's why I was probably unaware of the dangers. I used to walk through grass waist high without thinking for a moment what could have been lurking around my legs. Of course Australia has some of the most deadliest snakes in the world. I hate to think what would have happened if I'd been bitten by one! I'm sure I never would have made it back to camp. But I guess lady luck was always with me. I remember one particular day though when I was strolling through the bush on my own when all of a sudden this creature flew up into the air right in front of me, I must have surprised it as I got quite close to it before it flew off. However, it was me who was more surprised, I thought what the bloody hell was that! It had a strange funny shaped head and a huge wingspan. I'd never seen anything like it before and I wondered if I had stumbled on something that was thought to be extinct! A Teridactal perhaps! Anyway, when I got back to camp the Aussie's laughed when I described the prehistoric bird I had seen, they said "Oh, you mean a Brush Turkey, they're quite common out here" So my hopes of a rare discovery were totally dashed. I spotted another one a few days later and the Swedish guy tried to shoot it with his rifle. I thought it would be impossible to miss it because of its size, but somehow he did! I think if he had succeeded we would have been eating Turkey for the next couple of weeks!

On one of our days off we decided to go fishing as there was a creek not too far from the camp. There was me, Les and the Swedish guy. We didn't have a fishing rod but we made do with a few lines and hooks. I'd never been fishing in my life before so I wasn't very optimistic about catching anything. However it wasn't very long before I got a tug! I started to pull in the line but whatever it was it was too strong for me on my own so Les helped me. I thought this must be a really large fish and I had visions of a nice meal at the end of this. After quite a struggle we managed to haul it out of the water and onto the bank, but the thought of the nice meal soon disappeared when we saw what we had caught..... It was a bloody Turtle! We managed to get the hook out of its mouth and back into the water it went, and I don't think I got another bite after that.

When I first arrived in the bush, I notified the Army of my address, the same as I did when I first got to Renmark.

I think I had been working in the bush for about 10 weeks and I still hadn't had any word from the Army so I assumed my birth date hadn't been picked out, and therefore I wouldn't be going in the Army. However not long after, Jim the foreman brought the mail back from St Lawrence and to my surprise there amongst my usual mail was an official looking envelope. When I opened the letter, I was gobsmacked! The so-called million to one chance had happened and I was called up! But that was subject to a medical examination. Up to this point I had been in Australia for just more than six months, and in that time I had spent about three months picking grapes in South Australia and about the same amount of time in the Bush in Queensland. The rest of the time I had been travelling so I had no idea what to expect from the call-up. I started thinking maybe Army life might work out alright for me, although I had no idea then that the Australian troops were already fighting in Vietnam. However, before anything else I had to pass the medical and that was to be held in Rockhampton which was a small town about 50 miles away from the camp. There wasn't any public transport to get me to Rockhampton so I had to hitchhike. So on the day of the medical the rest of the guys went to work and I was left behind. I boiled some hot water, filled the tub and had a soak in a lovely hot bath. There was only one road leading to Rockhampton and that went right past the camp, so it wasn't long before I caught a lift. When I got to Rockhampton I headed straight to the nearest pub, I had a couple of beers and then made my way to the medical centre. At this point I'd like to remind you that the year was 1965 and the music world was buzzing with four lads from Liverpool, England, they were of course The Beatles. For some reason I thought that a small town in North Queensland wouldn't be as up to date as the rest of the world as far as the music scene was concerned, but how wrong could I be? I arrived at the medical centre and was shown into a room, the young girl asked me to remove my shirt for my chest X ray. Underneath my shirt I was wearing a T shirt (not a vest) which I had bought in Liverpool before I left for Australia. On the T shirt were the words "Liverpool Beat City, The Cavern Club" and the four Beatles' faces. The young girl heard my Liverpool accent and being quick put two and two together and said are you from Liverpool? Yes I said and that seemed to cause a bit of excitement and when another girl came in they ended up squabbling over who should X ray my chest! They asked did I know any of the Beatles or if I had ever met them. I thought for a few seconds and said to myself I don't suppose it will do any harm to tell a porky! So I told them I was Ringo's cousin, I chose Ringo because he has a small nose like me ha ha! When I was leaving, I threw my T shirt to the girls and left them fighting over it! If it's survived all this time, it's probably worth a few bob today. Once my medical was out of the way I spent the night in Rockhampton and the following day I hitchhiked back to camp.

All I had to do now is wait to see if I passed the medical. I thought it best not to tell my Mother at this stage just incase I failed the medical.

It was a few days later I received a letter from home telling me that one of my mates, Vic Knobbs had just emigrated to Australia and was living in Melbourne.

So after some discussions me and Les decided to pack in our jobs and head back to Melbourne to join up with Vic.

Me and my Afro hairstyle.
There were no barbers in the bush.
(The Bush Queensland)

Practicing my rifle skills
before I go into the Army.
(The Bush Queensland)

CHAPTER FIVE

FLYING DOWN TO MELBOURNE

After saying our goodbyes to the guys in the camp we headed to St Lawrence and stayed overnight in the same pub as we did the night we had arrived. The following morning we boarded the train for Mackay and once there got another train to Brisbane. By this time we had well and truly had enough of train journeys because up to that point we must have travelled more than 2500 miles by train. The journey from Brisbane to Melbourne would take about 12 hours but if we went by plane it would take less than two hours so we decided to fly from Brisbane to Melbourne.

Les and I had only flown once before and that was the journey from England to Australia. However, the planes we had travelled on to Australia had propellers and this meant that after takeoff we gained height gradually in stages. The plane from Brisbane to Melbourne had jet engines and I wasn't prepared for the take off. As the plane roared along the runway and took off suddenly it felt as though it went up vertically like a rocket. It gave us one hell of a fright and I think at that moment we wished we were back on a train! However, all was well once we levelled out and we were up above the clouds. The rest of the flight passed by quite quickly and we soon touched down safely in Melbourne and headed to the address we had been told Vic was staying at. It was a boarding house called The Towers and it was in the suburbs of Melbourne called Kew. We found out his room number and knocked on his door. When he opened the door, he was really surprised to see us as he had heard we were in Queensland. Anyway we told him what we had been up to since we arrived in Australia and he filled us in on all the latest news from home. We ended up talking away until the early hours.

The next day we went to see the landlady of The Towers - Mrs Duncan - we told her we had just arrived from Queensland to see

Vic and asked if she had any rooms for us. She gave us a large room on the ground floor that had four single beds and Vic was able to move into it with me and Les.

I asked Mrs Duncan if it would be all right if we had a bit of a reunion party in our room and invite some of the other residents. She said it would be ok as long as it didn't go on too late. So Les and me went out and bought all the booze and food.

There were about a dozen of us at the party but I remember we all had a good time. I started chatting up this young girl, Cheryl, who turned out to be the 16-year-old niece of Mrs Duncan. We seemed to hit it off straight away and from then on we started going out together.

After I had got over the effects of the party and my head was clear I remembered to notify the Army once again of my new address.

Les and I still had money left over from our last job so we didn't need to look for work straight away. However, we still had to pay for our digs, and our meals so we knew our money wouldn't last forever. We didn't want to make the same mistake as last time by running out of money.

So, we decided to look for a job as there seemed to be plenty of work around. It wasn't long before I got a job in the parks and gardens. It wasn't a bad job when you where out and about attending to different areas in the city, but unfortunately most of the time I was based in a type of garden centre, and the work involved planting bulbs and putting tiny seeds in boxes. It was so boring! The only thing that I looked forward to was playing table tennis at lunchtime. Back home I had always considered myself a decent sort of player, and at the garden centre there were a few good players too, so we used to have some good sessions each day.

It was always good fun until one day someone suggested playing for money and that's when it got out of hand. I used to hold my own with most of them except for one guy who had my number so to speak and he used to beat me nearly all the time. One day I ended up owing him £5 which might not seem a lot in today's money but in those days it was quite a bit. At the time I didn't have enough to pay him but he said I could pay him at the end of the week when I got my wages.

Anyway, that day back at the boarding house I picked up my mail and once again amongst my usual letters was that official looking envelope. So, this was it. I said to myself "have I passed my medical? Am I going in the Army?" When I opened the envelope I remember I had butterflies in my stomach and as I read the letter the words jumped out at me "REPORT FOR NATIONAL SERVICE".. The date was 29th September 1965.

My first thought was I've been given a clean bill of health and my second was how am I going to explain to my Mother that the million to one chance had happened and I was joining the Army! Anyway I wrote and told her the news and she replied that she was disappointed as it meant that I would be away from home longer that I had intended. There wasn't any mention of Vietnam at that point as I was still unaware of what was going on.

However, on the good side I was glad I could pack in the boring job at the garden centre and I wouldn't have to look around for another one. So, I was actually looking forward to Army life.

The next day I went to work and gave my notice in and I made arrangements to pick my wages up. However, there was still the little matter of the £5 that I owed the guy for losing to him at table tennis. He wasn't about when I went in for my wages, although I knew where he was working, but I'm ashamed to say I did a runner and welched on the bet. I suspect once he realised I'd pissed off he called me all the Pommy Bastard's under the sun, and I can't say I blame him either.

Back at the boarding house the day came when I was due to leave. I said goodbye to Les and Vic and gave Cheryl a kiss and said I would write to her. Mrs Duncan kindly said she would always have a room for me whenever I was on leave.

CHAPTER SIX

ARMY LIFE BEGINS!

It was 29th September 1965 and life in the Army was about to begin. I was told to report to an Army establishment near to Flinders Street Station in Melbourne city centre. I knew roughly where it was so headed off in what I thought was the right direction. I spotted a guy walking along carrying a holdall so I asked him if he knew where the Army place was, he said he did and it turned out that he was going there too. It turned out that he was a "Nasho" (National Serviceman) like me. His name was Lloyd Anstey and from that very first day and throughout our Army service we become very close friends.

We arrived at the Army establishment and met up with the rest of the Nasho's. We had a quick medical check and when everyone was accounted for we boarded a fleet of Army buses and off we went.

We were told that we were going to Puckapunyal Army barracks which was about 60 miles north. I thought Puckapunyal was a strange name for a place, and I found out later that it is an Aboriginal word that means "valley of the winds". I found out that the place lived up to its name. The hot winds would burn your face and crack your lips.

Army life started just as I had imagined it would. It was just like I've seen many times in the movies. We all lined up in our civvies, suitcases in hand and the Sergeant saying "Right you horrible lot, you're in the Army now!"

We put our suitcases into our billet and went to the Q-Store to get our Army kit. We then changed out of our civvies and into Jungle Greens. When we received the famous Aussie Slouch hat, I was a bit surprised to see that it was the same type that I was given as a trainee Shunter except this was brown instead of blue.

To make it look like an Army hat we had to soak the top of it in a bucket of water, put a dent in it, and then shape it. One of the Corporals made us all laugh when he said "Shape it so it looks like a Cow's C**t"

During our 12 weeks basic training I got to know the Aussie's properly for the first time. I got on really well with them and found them to be a great bunch of blokes. Of course, they used to take the piss out of my Scouse accent, but there was never any malice in it and I made a lot of good friends.

But you always get someone who doesn't take to you. I remember a time I had a bit of a set to with a guy, nothing too serious just a bit of a disagreement, but not long afterwards I had £20 stolen from my bedside cabinet and I was convinced that this bloke had taken it, although I didn't have any proof. What really upset me most about it was I was going to send that £20 to my Mother so that she could by herself something nice. £20 in those days was more than a week's wages.

I told the guys what had happened so they knew there was a thief in our midst. One of the guys offered to lend me £20 when he found out who it was meant for, his name was Bob White, he was also a Pom but he was an Australian citizen. I took up his offer and couldn't thank him enough.

I had to report the theft to the Captain and I was summoned to his office. When I walked in, he was sitting behind his desk and I stood to attention in front of him. He looked at me, waited a few seconds and said "Recruit Ponting, when you walk into my office try keeping your thumb closer to the palm of your hand when you salute me". I looked at him a bit confused and wondered what he meant until the penny dropped, I had forgotten to salute him, so he was taking the piss! I gave him a belated salute and he said "That's better, I believe you had £20 stolen from your room", he said. "Yes Sir", I replied. "Well, I should put you on a charge for leaving money lying around however, you don't expect to be robbed by one of your comrades, so we'll let the matter drop, but if you find out who took your money I will turn a blind eye if you give him a good hiding", he said. "Thank you Sir" I replied.

My Mum received the £20 thanks to Bob and I also sent my Dad a carton of cigarettes as they were a lot cheaper than back home. I got a big thank you from my Mother in her next letter and thanks from Dad for the ciggies, although Dad was grateful he told me not to send him any more as he had to pay import duty on them and that meant between us we actually ended up paying more for them. By this time we were well in to our basic training which would last 12 weeks.

Every morning a bugler would sound for Reveille at 06:00 hours. That felt like the middle of the night to me because I had never had a job where I had to get up that early. In the past no matter what time I had to be in work I would always leave it to the last minute to get up and dressed. I never bothered with breakfast, I used to get out of bed and within 10 minutes I'd be on my way to work. So when the bugler sounded, all the guys used to jump out of bed and line up for roll call. When my name was called, I would still be lying in bed. This didn't go down well with the rest of the guys, they used to shout out "come on Scouse, get your fuckin' arse out here". We had to bring a sheet off our bed with us that was to make sure you stripped your bed so you would make it again properly. But I found a way around that! I used to take my pillow slip out instead. I would fold it over my arm and all through basic training the NCO's never twigged! Basic training was hard going but I enjoyed it because I was young and fit, even though I smoked at the time. But I even surprised myself one day when we went for a 10-mile cross country run and I finished in the first 20! I was always pretty good at gymnastics at school, I could do hand springs and flick flacks. I got on well with the PE Instructor Bombardier Hoader and I really enjoyed going over the assault course. I remember having a bet with a 2nd Lieutenant over who would finish the course first. I can't remember how much the bet was but I won the bet and he paid up, and it was a nice feeling to get one over on an officer.

I think one of the hardest endurance tasks I did was a 9-mile force march. It was really tough, especially as it was so hot. You had to run and march for 9 miles nonstop with your rifle. After we finished and I got back to camp I took my boots off and my feet were covered in blisters. My calf muscles were twice their size which was the only thing I was happy about because I've always had skinny legs! Unfortunately, the next day my legs were back to normal.

All the Corporals who trained us throughout our basic training gave us a really hard time, but that was only to be expected. However, they treated us all as equals and I must admit once our basic training was over I had a lot of respect for them. There was one Corporal though that I had my doubts about. He didn't seem as hard as the others and not as authoritative. I thought he seemed more suited to some sort of desk job. His name slips my mind, but one day my opinion of him changed. We were out at the firing range and we had to throw our first live grenades. Me and another soldier stood behind the sandbags pulled the pins out of the grenades and threw them simultaneously and ducked down. A few second later one explosion happened, but no second explosion. We waited for about 5 minutes but still no explosion. That meant that someone had to walk over to the unexploded grenade and place a charge next to it. I thought that would take a lot of nerve and there was still a good chance it would explode. To my surprise the Corporal who I had my doubts about calmly walked over and placed a charge next to the grenade and it was safely detonated. After that I had a lot of respect for him.

As our basic training was coming to an end, all the attention was centred around our passing out parade. It was a big occasion for all of us and most of the guy's parents and friends would be there to watch them. Of course, my parents couldn't be there but it didn't stop me from feeling very proud.

41

The passing out parade went really well and afterwards we were given two weeks leave which meant we were off over Christmas and New Year.

3787715 Recruit Ponting D.L.
My first photo taken during basic training.

Me in bed writing my first letter home.

John, me and Lloyd
enjoying a celebration drink
after our passing out parade.

CHAPTER SEVEN

FIRST LEAVE

Now that our 12-week basic training was over everyone was looking forward to our first leave.

I headed back to the boarding house in Melbourne to see Vic and Cheryl, Les had left Melbourne a month earlier and had gone to work in Perth, Western Australia. When I left the Army camp one of my mates, John Madden said to look him up when I was on leave. He said that his Dad had a boat and if I wanted I could come along and have a day out with them. So I took him up on his offer and we had a really good time sailing around Port Phillip Bay.

I had other good days out as well but unfortunately it didn't last. Something happened that would have a lasting effect on me. It was a couple of days before I was due back at camp. Me and Vic had heard about a barbecue being held at Richmond which wasn't too far from where we lived. So we thought we'd go along. We got there about 6pm and you had to pay to get in, the price included food and drinks. There were quite a lot of people there, there was a bloke playing an accordion and everyone seemed to be having a really good time. The party was still in full swing at midnight but me and Vic had had enough to drink and we decided to leave. We'd only gone a short distance up the road when a group of about 10 young guys started following us. We didn't pay much attention to them as we were quite drunk and thought nothing of it. That is until some of them overtook us and then turned to face us and the rest remained behind us, we were now completely surrounded. Then for no apparent reason they beat the shit out of us. We were punched, kicked and blows came in from all angles. I tried fighting back, but it's no good when you're pissed, I was just hitting thin air. The next thing I remember was waking up in the gutter with Vic lying next to me. I don't know how long we'd been unconscious but the gang had disappeared. I remember two sailors helping us into a taxi. When we got back to the boarding house, I helped Vic inside because his eyes were so swollen they'd closed over and he couldn't see a thing. Fortunately in time Vic would not suffer any long lasting effects. I wasn't so fortunate however. I had deep cuts and abrasions to my face, my nose was full of blood and my lips were swollen to twice their normal size, but what was to be a permanent reminder was that three of my front teeth had been knocked clean out and a fourth was bent right back. I was devastated because I've always taken pride in my teeth.

When we woke up the next morning, we were still in a sorry state. I made my way to the bathroom down the corridor and I bumped right into Cheryl. The look of shock on her face said it all. She was really upset and looked concerned about me. I remember thinking if Cheryl had been with me that night things might have turned out differently and perhaps it might not have happened at all. I remember feeling guilty too for not spending more time with Cheryl on my first leave.

What happened to me and Vic didn't change the good opinion I still had for the Australian people. Unfortunately, you get cowardly thugs in every society.

When I arrived back at camp and the sergeant saw the state I was in, he sent me to the Regimental Aid Post (RAP). The Dentist examined my mouth and looked at the remaining front tooth and told me that it would have to come out too. So now, my four front teeth were missing and I looked like Dracula!

Our company was due to go on a 3-day exercise in the Bush, but I was told I couldn't go because I still had open cuts on my face and they could attract too many flies. So I was left behind in the barracks as the rest of the guys went out in the bush. I spent the next three days lying on my bed reading and writing letters. Of course I never told my Mother what had happened to my teeth.

It wasn't too long before I was fitted with dentures, but as soon as I put them in my mouth I thought how the hell am I going to get used to these, and if the truth be known throughout the following years I never really did.

Note: In 1998 I paid a lot of money on dental work to my teeth. It meant I no longer have to wear dentures. The result is permanent and I can brush my teeth like they are all my own.

From the right standing: Me, Don, Lloyd and friends having a drink in a Melbourne pub.

Geoff, Vic, Macca, Kevin, Me and Mick having a party at a friends house.

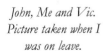

John, Me and Vic. Picture taken when I was on leave.

45

CHAPTER 8

7 RAR - MY NEW BATTALION

After basic training I decided to join the Infantry. I joined the 7th Royal Australian Regiment (7 RAR). It was a new infantry battalion consisting mainly of conscripts. I was still stationed at Puckapunyal but in a different area than before. I persuaded my mate Lloyd Anstey to join me, although I think he favoured the Royal Australian Electrical and Mechanical Engineers (RAEME), but I convinced him it would be more of an adventure in the Infantry, and as it turned out, it was, but not the way that I meant.

At this point we all knew what was going on in Vietnam. But I still didn't think any of us really expected that we would end up there. We were no longer recruits, we now had the rank of Private and we were about to start our Corps training.

Joining a new battalion meant making new friends and one of them was Don Castagna who lived in Reservoir, a suburb of Melbourne, not far from where I was living in Kew.

When I told Don I was staying at the boarding house, he said "why don't you come and stay at my place next time we're on leave". So, a few weeks later we went to his home and I was introduced to his Mum and Dad, Sister Val (19) and twins Robert and Julie (12). I knew straight away that they were a lovely family, and from then on I was treated as one of the family too. The next time we were on leave after that was at the end of March. It was close to my 21st Birthday and it was also Val's 19th birthday, and a party had been organised for Val. Family and friends arrived at the family home and some of our Army mates were invited too. When it was time to blow out the candles on her birthday cake, I noticed what was written on the cake. It said "Happy Birthday Val" and underneath was "Congratulations Derek on your 21st Birthday". I was really surprised, because I had no idea, and the surprise didn't stop there, there were presents from my Army pals and also from people I hardly knew. They also gave me a large wooden 21st Key which opened up and inside everyone had signed it and wished me all the best.

I wrote to my Mother and told her all about what the family had done for me for my Birthday. Mother wrote back asking me to thank them from her and Dad for giving me such a special day. She even admitted to having a little cry too.

Another close friend that I made in 7 RAR was Kevin Leder. He made life in the Army much easier for me, because he could always make me laugh. I remember on one particular exercise when we'd walked for miles and miles and we hadn't had a break in what seemed like ages. We were all knackered. Finally we were told we could have a 10 minute rest (Smoko). After what seemed like only a couple of minutes, we were given the order to move on again. The Sergeant came over to us and said "On your feet", everyone jumped up except Kevin. The Sergeant walked over to him and stood right over him and said "that means you as well Private Leder, get on your fuckin' feet now". Kevin looked up at him and said "I can't Sarg", "why not?" said the Sergeant, "Cos I've only got stumps left Sarg!" It was the way he said it that had me falling about laughing. He would sometimes get me into trouble as well, I remember this particular morning when we were out on exercise, both of us were in our dugout and we were just about to stand down to have breakfast, when he dared me to throw a thunder flash grenade from the pit. Foolishly I picked one up, pulled the pin out and threw it! The explosion brought the Sergeant running over to us "Who the fuck threw that?" I owned up, but I couldn't very well say that he dared me to do it, so I said "I thought I saw the enemy in the bushes Sarg", he said "don't take the piss Scouse, you know nobody's out there!" I didn't really expect him to believe me and he gave me a right bollocking and rightly so! Even some of the other guys called me a few names because of what I did. It meant that all of us had to stand-to longer than we should have! All that just because Kevin dared me! But me and Kev still had a laugh about it afterwards. Making me laugh so much was probably the reason I used to lose concentration. Quite often if the NCO's asked me questions and Kevin was next to me I'd always say "Can you repeat the question please?" So I don't think I came over as the brightest of people, and one day I confirmed what they thought about me. I was assigned to clean the Captain's office and the cabinet that contained the personal files was unlocked, so I decided to look at my file!

What I read came as a bit of a surprise to me. It said *"generally confused, below average intelligence, some potential NCO!"* I thought the last bit didn't say much for our present NCOs considering the fact that they thought I was thick! Anyway, whatever they thought of me the time I spent with Kevin made Army life a lot more fun.

Another one of our exercises took place at Tallarook. It wasn't far from Puckapunyal but I remember the weather being very cold. It was still very windy, but the chill factor made it seem even colder. I hadn't felt so cold since I left home, some of the guys came over to me and asked if it got this cold in England, I told them that yes of course it did, but I felt the cold just as much as they did because I had been in Australia for over a year and I was used to the warm weather. One of the guys made us laugh when he said, "how come we are training in freezing cold weather, have they moved Vietnam to the South Pole?"

It wasn't all work. We did have some time to relax. We had a billet near us that was converted into a games room where we could play chess, darts, cards and table tennis. Playing table tennis again made me think of what had happened at the garden centre. Had I learned my lesson? Well, I was still beating most of the guys but once again someone had my number and that was my mate Kevin Leder, except this time I had the sense not to play him for money. However, one day I asked another soldier Ian Gibson, who I hadn't seen play table tennis, did he want to play best of three games for money. I can't remember now how much it was for, but he won the first game, I won the second and yes you've guessed it, he won the third game! Obviously I still hadn't learnt my lesson! One again I got my comeuppance and this time I couldn't do a runner even if I had wanted to!

We also had a large outdoor swimming pool at Pucka' to relax in, and I used to spend a lot of time in the pool, especially on hot days. Once our Corps training was over the rules were relaxed and at weekends you were allowed to have friends and family visit you.

I remember one weekend a couple of my civvy mates, Vic and Gerry came up to see me.

Me keeping warm wearing scarf and combat jacket.

Me relaxing with a comic while on exercise.

Close friends Kevin and me.

*Close friends
Lloyd and me.*

Me, Lloyd and Trevor taking a rest after a long slog.
The long faces say it all!

Lunchtime. Me opening a tin of meat.

Gerry, me and Vic.
They came on a day visit to 7 RAR Barracks.

Me, returning from a swim in friend's car.
The car belonged to Gary, who crashed it shortly afterwards and tragically died.

CHAPTER 9

CANUNGRA AND INGLEBURN

Now that our Corps training was over and we'd been on a few exercises, next up was our jungle training. We had to leave Puckapunyal, Victoria and travel up north to a place called Canungra, Queensland. I think it was sometime in July 1966 and a month earlier the first large contingent of National Servicemen from 6 RAR, had left for a 12-month tour of duty in Vietnam, so they weren't due back until June 1967. There was a rumour that our battalion 7 RAR was to replace them when their tour was over. I thought if that's the case I wouldn't be sent over to Vietnam, or a very slim chance of being sent, because I would only have a short time left to serve in the Army. However, what didn't cross my mind was that reinforcements might be required.

I remember getting a letter from my Mother about this time. She had obviously found out about Australia's involvement in the war because she asked me if I would be going to Vietnam. I wrote back and told her about the situation as I knew it and I think I must have given her the impression that I wouldn't be going. Of course, a few weeks later that would all change.

Anyway our jungle training had to come first. On our arrival at Canungra I got off to the worst possible start. We lined up and we were given orders on what to do and what not to do. One of the things you couldn't do was sit or lie on your bed before lights out. Anyone who did would be put on a charge. Now for some reason this order didn't register with me or perhaps I never heard it, I don't really know. Anyway, once I'd put my gear in the locker I sat down on my bed. Straight away an Officer walked in and gave me a real bollocking. I tried to explain to him that I never knew about the order, but he wasn't having any of it and he put me on a charge. I got three days confined to barracks (CB).

It couldn't have happened at a worse time, because it was the start of the weekend and all the other guys were off into town. I had to stay behind and the CSM had me marching around the parade ground. After that I had to report to the duty Sergeant every hour, and each time I had to be dressed in different clothes. First I had to wear Battle Dress, then Jungle Greens, then PE Kit! I had to do this for three consecutive nights and all because I had sat on my bed. It really pissed me off!

Things didn't go right for me either when it came to our first training exercise. It happened during a tactical river crossing. We had to cross from one side of the riverbank to the other and we were told that total silence had to be observed at all times. We had to act as though we were in the middle of enemy territory. We had to take our boots and clothes off, put them inside a poncho and rest our rifles on top. We then had to push the poncho into the water and quietly swim to the other side. Simple enough? Except nobody told me how cold the water was. I remember it was a lovely, sunny morning and I was expecting the water to be warm, so the temperature took me completely by surprise. As I entered the water it took my breath away and as a result my dentures shot out and promptly sank to the bottom of the river! Well, I forgot all about keeping silent and shouted out "Oh Shit!" Immediately the Captain on the riverbank told us to be quiet, I shouted back "But Sir, I've lost my bloody teeth" and with that all the guys on the bank, including the Captain fell about laughing. I tried a few times to find them by diving under the water, but without success. So, I was glad to see the back of Canungra and head back to Puckapunyal.

The fateful river crossing which claimed my dentures.
Location: Canungra QLD, 1966.

We hadn't been back very long when we heard some terrible news. Six Battalion had been in a major battle with the North Vietnamese Army. 18 Australian soldiers had been killed and 21 seriously injured. Delta Company suffered the most casualties and eleven of the 18 soldiers that had been killed were conscripts. That brought home to me the fact that we were just as much in the forefront as the regular soldiers.

It was a heavy loss for the Australians in their first major battle of the war, but the enemy suffered a lot more casualties. It was estimated that the North Vietnamese lost more than 200 men with many more injured.

It became known as the Battle of Long Tan and I believe there have been a few books written about it. One book I would highly recommend is "Long Tan and Beyond" written by Lt Col Charles Mollison. He describes the battle in detail and soldiers recount their stories of what happened. It also tells about other battles that took place during the war, between 1966-67.

I'm not sure if it was as a direct result of the Long Tan battle, but shortly afterwards we were told that some of us would be going to the reinforcement centre in Ingleburn, near Sydney.

When I was told I would be going to Ingleburn, I wondered what my Mother's reaction was going to be when I told her. I was hoping that she hadn't heard the news about the Australian soldiers who had died during the Battle of Long Tan, as I knew it would only make her worry even more. Anyway, I wrote and told her what to expect.

Dear Mam,

The reason I'm writing this letter so soon after my last one, is because I've just been told that I'm being posted to Ingleburn. I'll be stationed at the reinforcement centre, which means it looks like I'll be going to Vietnam after all. I'm not sure how long I'll be at the centre. It could be weeks or even months, I don't really know, I'll just have to wait and see. I'll be leaving quite a few good mates behind in 7 RAR, but I don't think it will be that long before they join me.

So Mam, don't send anymore letters here. I'll send you my new address as soon as I know it, so,

Look after yourself, and don't worry, your loving Son,

Derek xxxx

Memories...

I thought once my Mother received this letter it would come as quite a shock to her, and I suppose it was the start of her worries. Anyway, once I arrived at the Reinforcement Centre and settled in, it was a case of being briefed and making new friends once again.

One of the friends I made was Adrian (Rod) Roderick. He was also a NASHO and like myself a Pom. He was born in London, but he was an Australian citizen. We had a couple of weekends off while we were at the centre and as it was only a short taxi drive into Sydney we took advantage of it. We went to Kings Cross where all the night clubs are. I think we ended up in the Crazy Horse Cabaret club. They had Drag artists on and I remember it was a fantastic show and it was one of the best nights out I ever had in Australia.

Me and Rod at a Sydney Night Club, nice teeth on Rod - shame I couldn't show mine, but they are lying at the bottom of a Queensland river!

Dear Mam,

I'm sorry I haven't written to you sooner and I'm sorry this letter will have to be a brief one.

We've just been informed we're going to Vietnam in the next couple of days. As you can imagine, we're all running round getting our gear packed and sorting everything out before we go.

When we fly out, we've been told our first stop is in Manila which is the capital of the Philippines. Ask my dad to show you where it is on the map. We get a two-day break when we get there, so we'll make sure we have a good time, as we won't know when we'll get another one.

I'll write to you as soon as possible with my new address once I've settled in. Look after yourself and try not to worry, I'll be okay.

Your loving Son
Derek xxxx

Memories...

This letter I wrote to my Mother was probably the one she least wanted to receive.

It was to confirm that I was leaving for Vietnam. I remember having mixed feelings about going. I was apprehensive but at the same time quite excited, and I think that was the case with most of the other guys too. When we were at the Q store waiting to be issued with our gear, we were acting like a gang of school kids. We were making a hell of a noise, pushing and shoving one another and making complete fools of ourselves. Finally the Staff Sergeant behind the counter seen his arse and blew his top. For reasons known only to him, he singled me out and had a real go at me in front of the guys. He was like a schoolteacher telling a pupil off only much worse! He said to me, "what the fuck do you think you're playing at? Get to the back of the queue and keep your mouth shut". I said "it wasn't only me making a noise". "I don't give a shit", he said "and when you speak to me call me by my rank!" It had gone very quiet and everyone was looking at me, I remember thinking, "I'm off to Vietnam in a couple days and who knows I mightn't even come back, so I'm going to have a go back at him and sod the consequences! So, I said "Don't you speak to me like that, I'm not some raw recruit you can treat like shit and when you speak to me call me by my rank too".

He could have quite easily put me on a charge for insubordination, but to my surprise he replied in a calm voice, "Ok, I just want you all to keep the noise down that's all". I felt I had restored a little bit of pride and I no longer felt humiliated in front to the guys. Some of them even said afterwards, "good on yer Scouse", which made me really feel a whole lot better.

When we left Australia we didn't fly directly to Vietnam, we stopped off first in Manila, in the Philippines. When we arrived at the Airport, I got into a taxi with four other guys and we were taken to a hotel in the heart of the city. Our taxi driver told us that he was going to be our guide and chauffeur for the two days we would be staying in Manila and that it wouldn't cost us anything as the Army was paying his fee, which was great!

Over the next two days and nights the driver took us to restaurants, night clubs and on sightseeing tours. We got to know the Driver quite well, his name was Victor Soon and I'll always remember his hospitality and friendly manner.

Me (far right) with some of the guys from the Reinforcement Centre and Escort Girls,
Our Guide Victor Soon (in front)

CHAPTER 10

ARRIVING IN VIETNAM

Dear Mam,

Just a quick letter to let you know we arrived in Vietnam safely and we're now at the Australian Task Force base in Nui Dat. It's in a rubber plantation about 120 miles from Saigon. Since we've been here, things have been very quiet, you wouldn't think there was a war going on. There's a small village close by to us called Hoa Long. You have to feel sorry for the people living there, they are very poor and their homes are wooden shacks.

The weather here is very humid at the moment, so I got one of my mates to cut my hair. Sorry I did because he cut it that short I looked like Yul Brynner. Not to worry though, nobody takes any notice of you out here, and besides it helps to keep you cool.

The rain is torrential out here aswell. It was quite funny the other day because we were having our breakfast in the canteen when the heavy rain caused a small river to rush through and swept our table away.

I've been told that letters to and from England have to go via Australia, so I think our mail might take a little longer to reach one another, but don't worry I'll write as often as possible. We had a really good time in Manila on our way over here. It's just a pity we couldn't have spent more time there.

I'll close now Mam, so look after yourself.

Write soon,

Your Loving Son,
Derek xxxx

Memories...

As we were flying over Vietnam I looked out of the window of the plane and saw the snakelike shape of the Mekong Delta, and wondered what was in store for us all.

Once we arrived at Saigon Airport we were met by a few Aussies and as we were being introduced there was a loud explosion which didn't sound like it was too far away.

We found out later that someone had set a bomb off near to a hotel. I thought at the time was this the start of things to come? Anyway, we were taken to an American Army base which was about a mile or so outside the city of Saigon. After we had settled in and been briefed, we were told we could have a night out in Saigon. We were accompanied by the same Aussies who met us at the airport, one of whom was fluent in Vietnamese. It was just like being back in the Philippines, plenty of bars and plenty of girls which meant we all had too much to drink, which probably explained how stupid I acted near the end of the night. I was standing at the bar having a drink when I noticed one of the bar girls was staring and pointing at me while she was talking to one of the other bar girls and then they started giggling. At first I thought they were laughing at the gap in my mouth were I had lost my teeth, so I felt a bit embarrassed. I asked the Aussie bloke to translate what they were saying about me and he said "Do you really want to know?" I said "why, is it that bad?" - "No not really" he said, one of them wants you to spend the night with her because she's turned on by your big nose and curly hair." I thought, shall I take that as a compliment then! All Vietnamese people have straight hair and small noses, so I guess I was some sort of novelty for her. The Aussie interpreter told me it wouldn't be wise if I stayed behind, but if I decided to then I should make sure that I was back at Camp before anyone noticed I was missing. So against my better judgement I spent the night with her and after we had done the business, we fell asleep. In the early hours she woke me up and I could see she had a worried look on her face and she gestured to me to hide under the bed. I could hear people talking and making a noise outside the window which overlooked the alleyway. For all I knew it could have been a jealous boyfriend or even worse the Viet Cong! However, to my relief nothing came of it, but looking back, how the hell could I have been so stupid! To stay on my own on the very first night in Vietnam! What a plonker! So early in the morning I left the room and went outside and flagged down an American Army truck outside that took me to the camp and luckily for me I hadn't been missed. If my memory serves me right, after that we travelled in a Caribu Army plane to Vung Tau, which was the main Australian Logistic camp. Once we arrived there, we were issued with our rifles, webbing and ammunition. It seemed quite strange receiving "live" ammo for the first time other than being on the firing range. It made me stop and think, this is now for real and we would no longer be firing blanks! As a Rifleman whenever you went out on patrol you always carried seven magazines of ammo, three in each pouch of your webbing and one on your rifle. 140 rounds in all and two hand grenades. We left Vung Tau in Army trucks and travelled to Nui Dat which was situated in a rubber plantation. It was to be our home base for most of the time we would spend in Vietnam.

***

In this first letter from Vietnam I mentioned how sorry I felt for the people living in the village of Hoa Long, because of the conditions they had to put up with. I remember the first time I went to the village. I was in a small party that consisted of about seven of us which included an Officer and a Padre. I thought it unusual for a Padre to be with us. But I soon realised why when we stopped at a "house" which was a wooden shack. An old woman appeared at the door, she was very emotional and the Padre was comforting her. I saw the Officer hand the woman a large amount of money. Apparently, as we found out later, her husband had been accidentally killed by Australian forces. I assume the money was some sort of compensation, but I never found out how he died.

There was a large area of sand just outside the village and the Aussies used to pay the villagers to fill sand bags for us. There were also plenty of kids helping out too. So I don't think there were any schools in the nearby area.

***

Also mentioned in my first letter was the humidity and the torrential rain we had to contend with. Whenever you returned from a patrol you were always soaking wet, either due to the rain or sweat. All of us at some time or other would suffer from Tinea due to the weather conditions. It is a skin disease that itches like mad and mainly affects your crotch area. I had a bad case of it and I used to scratch it until I was red raw, and what with the heat and the sweat it used to sting like hell. But we were all in the same boat, so we just had to grin and bear it. Eventually, our bodies got accustomed to the conditions and with ointment we were given it managed to clear up.

CHAPTER 11

CREEPY CRAWLIES!

Dear Mam,

Thanks very much for your letter which I have just received.

It's nice to know everyone at home is keeping well, as it leaves me the same here. I was surprised to hear what you read in the paper about British people living in Australia don't have to register for National Service unless they've been there for at least two years. If that's correct, it means that I shouldn't have registered, and my call up was a mistake.

Well Mam, it's too late to do anything about it now, what's done is done and I'll just have to get on with it. But, to be honest Mam, I'm glad I'm in the Army because it's taught me a lot about myself and being in Vietnam has made me realise how lucky I am to have a home and a family like mine.

The Aussies are planning to put a big show on for us at Xmas. We've been told they've got some top entertainers from Australia coming over, so we're all looking forward to it. I'm sorry to hear you're still having cold weather back home. I sometimes wish we had a bit of English weather out here, because then we might not have to put up with mosquitoes', leeches and some of the other creepy crawlies.

I've had some photos taken recently, but think they have to be sent to Australia first to be developed. I'll send them to you when I get them back.

You asked what I wanted for Xmas, well Mam there's nothing I really need out here. Just send me a Christmas card and keep sending me your letters, that's all I need to cheer me up.

I'll sign off now Mam, so look after yourself and keep smiling, Your loving Son,

Derek xxx

Memories...

My Mother seemed to think I was called up by mistake. She had read that you had to have lived in Australia for two years before you were eligible for National Service. However, as I found out much later, that wasn't the case. All 20 year old British subjects had to register for national service, regardless of the time they'd been in Australia. The rule that you had to be a resident for at least two years before you were eligible for conscription only applied to foreign nationals. I've often wondered would I still have emigrated had I known there was a chance of being drafted into the Army and sent to Vietnam. I think that I still would have taken a chance, because I planned to work on the railways for about a year, get some money behind me, and then make my fortune Opal mining or gold prospecting. However, the Australian government had other plans for me.

As Christmas approached the entertainers arrived in Vietnam, and as promised we got the top artists from Australia who would perform for us. Names like Normie Rowe, Little Pattie, Ricky Starr and Lorraine Desmond. Okay perhaps they're not your everyday household names but don't forget this was more than 40 years ago and at the time they were big down under. The American's also had their own Christmas Show, they had entertainers such as Bob Hope, Eddie Fisher, Phyllis Diller and Ann-Margaret, but let's face it who's heard of them outside the USA!

Lorraine Desmond entertaining the Australian troops.

***

The leeches I mention were a real nuisance, every time you went out on patrol you could guarantee you had leeches for company.

It was amazing some of the places they used to get on your body before they started sucking your blood. They were quite thin which enabled them to somehow get inside your boots. Your feet would squelch when you were walking. At first you thought it was just sweat that is until you took your boots off and found your socks full of blood. But what was more amazing was, they could get inside your trousers and try to get down inside the pee-hole of your penis. We were advised by the Medics that if that happened the best way to get rid of one was to masturbate, no I'm not kidding! So, if anyone was ever caught in the act, it was a good excuse to say you had a leech!

It wasn't only leeches we had to put up with. I remember one day I was lying on the ground with my boots off having a doze, when I felt something crawl up inside my trouser leg and onto my thigh. I thought it was some sort of small insect so I just hit it with my hand and then I felt this terrific pain at the base of my thumb as though someone had stuck a knife into me. I immediately jumped up and then felt the same sharp pain in my thigh. At first I thought it was a snake, but as I dropped my trousers there it was..... a red scorpion and I had been stung twice by it. Now I've seen movies in the past where people have died when they've been stung by a scorpion, although the ones in the movies were always big and black. Anyway I wasn't taking any chances so I killed it with my boot and then ran with it to the first aid tent. After I was reassured I wasn't going to die of blood poisoning I was given some ointment and sent on my way. But my hand and leg were still sore about three days later.

The mosquitoes too were part of our everyday life. We had to take a tablet every day to prevent us getting malaria. However, some of the guys still caught it. I don't know how true it was but I heard a rumour that some of the guys stopped taking their tablets in the hope of catching malaria and being sent home. I believe at first that's what happened, but after a while those guys who caught malaria had to stay in Vietnam and spend about three weeks in hospital before being sent back to their unit.

CHAPTER 12

CHRISTMAS IN 'NAM - 1966

Dear Mam

I've just received your most welcome letter, I'm glad to hear everyone's still well back home, as it leaves me the same here. I'm sorry if my writing seems a little different than usual but it's 10.30 in the evening and the only light I've got is coming from the full moon. I shouldn't be writing this letter at all really because I'm on sentry duty, but don't worry I've got my mate who's next to me keeping a look out.

Well Mam I hope you enjoyed yourself over Xmas. I managed to have quite a few beers with the lads, and we all had a good time. At the moment we're patrolling and guarding Route 15 which is the road the Yankee convoys are using as they head up north to DMZ. It's an easy job and we get more time to relax. We'll be doing this until 12th January. At the end of January I'm due to take my R&R. I've been told I can take it in Hong Kong. However, I spoke to a few guys who have just come back from there and they said they spent a fortune, so I'm having second thoughts about going. I'm trying to save as much money as I can so we can have a good time when I get home. I'll probably stay in Vietnam and take my leave in Vung Tau which is right on the beach and it will be a lot cheaper too.

I got a nice surprise off Cheryl just before Xmas. She sent me a huge parcel which must have cost her quite a bit of money. It contained beer, tins of fruit, bars of chocolate and it even had a Xmas pudding in it aswell as lots of other things. She put a note in it which said "to the best fella in the world, wishing you a merry Xmas", I must admit it brought a lump to my throat.

I received a letter off Janet last week and she also said she's sent me a Xmas parcel, but as yet I haven't received it.

Anyway one thing for sure I'm really getting looked after while I'm out here.

Well Mam, I'll have to close now, so Happy New Year to you, my Dad, Brian and everyone back home. Look after yourself and have a good time and remember I'll be thinking of you all.

Your Loving Son

Derek

P.S. give Lassie a big hug for me.

Memories...

As I mentioned in this letter, I was on sentry duty when I was writing it. It probably wasn't a wise thing to do but as I said I had my mate next to me so it's not as bad as it sounds.

It was a full moon that night and I could just about see what I was writing but when the moon and stars weren't out it was pitch black and you couldn't see your hand in front of your face.

One night in the rubber plantation in Nui Dat I had a slight mishap. After a few drinks in the mess I was walking back to my tent which was about 100 yards away. It was an overcast night and once I had gone a few feet from the mess I couldn't see a thing. To avoid us getting lost in the dark communication cords had been set up around the camp, which you could hold onto to get safely from one place to another in the dark. On this particular night in question I set off to go back to my tent, I was holding onto the "comms cord" with one hand and my rifle in the other (your rifle went everywhere with you, even when you went for a shite) when suddenly the cord came to an end! I thought someone must have fallen on it and it had snapped or perhaps some practical joker cut it for a laugh! Anyway I felt around trying to feel for the other end but without success, so I headed towards what I thought was the right direction and the next thing I knew I fell four feet down into one of our gun pits. It gave me quite a shock, but I'd had a few drinks so I saw the funny side of it. I dusted myself off and set off once again only to disappear down another gun pit, or it might have been the same pit for all I knew! At that point I started thinking that if it had been cut deliberately I'd like to get my hands on the guy who had done it! But to be honest I still laughed about it when I eventually got back to my tent. However, if you think about the consequences of what might have happened that night, for instance if when I fell I'd had an AD (accidental discharge) of my rifle, it wouldn't have been anything to laugh about. Fortunately I got back to the tent relatively unscathed and none the worse for my ordeal.

I remember another time when I was on sentry duty, but this time I was on my own and it was during daytime. I was told by the Sergeant to relieve a soldier (Bill Byers) who was on sentry duty about 50 yds down this dirt track. The Sergeant pointed me in the right direction and I walked down the track a fair distance but I couldn't see any sign of Bill. I assumed he had gone back to camp and we'd probably passed each other without noticing because the jungle was quite dense. So I sat down cross legged with my rifle in my lap. After about 10 minutes had passed I heard a noise a few yards in front of me and noticed the bushes moving. I felt my heart starting to beat faster as I put my rifle to my shoulder and just as I was about to pull the trigger I saw Bill! It seemed incredible that we'd been sitting only a few yards apart and hadn't noticed each other. It also made me realise how close the Viet Cong could get to you without being seen. Anyway, after me and Bill had got over the shock we managed to have a laugh about it, but it could so easily have been a very different story. However, unfortunately for Bill he was still not out of danger from me, as you will read later on in the book.

71

On 'Operation Duck One' it was our job to patrol and guard Route 15 so that the American convoys could travel up North towards the DMZ. We had to make sure that the Viet Cong didn't attack them and stop them planting mines or booby traps.

The route of course was also used by civilians and every so often when we were resting up at the roadside, a scooter would pull up with a Vietnamese girl on the back and she would offer to have sex with you in the bushes. Although you would have been on a charge if you risked it, I still think some of the guys took them up on the offer. I suppose it was only natural for us to get sexually frustrated, we were all young guys and there was no sex available at the camp in Nui Dat. It was a case of waiting until you were on leave before any sex was available. I remember one of the guys at camp made a wanking machine. I was told it was like a small wooden shoebox which had a hole in one end where you put your willy and a handle on the side that when it was turned rotated a lot of feathers inside. I was told that the Padre found out about it and confiscated it! The rumour was that a strange noise was coming from the Padre's tent each night. Well, they say God works in mysterious ways, don't they? Sex was available in Vung Tau, that's where the Aussies and Americans spent their R and C leave.

I recall a time when I hadn't been in Vietnam all that long, about a week I think and I was told to ride shotgun on an Army truck to Vung Tau. There was just me and the driver in the truck. As we approached Vung Tau we were travelling behind a small Vietnamese vehicle. It was the type you see all over Vietnam that are used as taxis, but they don't have a steering wheel, instead they have handle bars. Actually, I think they are scooters with a shell around them and they seat about six people.

A typical means of transport used in and around Vung Tau.

Anyway, there was this pretty Vietnamese girl sitting at the back of this vehicle and she made a gesture to us by making a fist with one hand and then tapping the side of it with the palm of her other hand. To us soldiers that meant only one thing "bum bum" (sex). When the vehicle stopped, we pulled up behind it and the girl got off and crossed over the road. My driver said "hang on here, I won't be long" and followed her which left me on my own in the truck. Although an attack from the Viet Cong would have been very unlikely, because we were just outside Vung Tau, but I had only been in Vietnam a short time and I was a bit naive. I remember thinking what if I had been attacked and later had to explain to an officer where the driver was at the time. I would have had to have said "Oh, he just popped over the road Sir for a quick shag."

Anyway, once we arrived in Vung Tau the local kids were there to greet us. They were like kids the world over, trying to find ways of making a quick buck. Although they could be cheeky at times, they were also quite funny. They called the Aussies "Uc da li", which I was told roughly translated means big red rat. I don't think they meant anything bad by it, they were just referring to the red Kangaroo that was painted on all our military vehicles and helicopters.

If the kids liked you or you bought something off them they would say "You number one Uc da li" and if they didn't like you they would say "you number 10". One of the ways they used to make money was by cleaning your boots. I remember this particular day when one of the kids made me laugh. He was probably about 10 or 11 years old and he hit on the idea of saying "I polish boots for free". Obviously, thinking once he had cleaned them, they'd pay him anyway. So this kid stopped a big black GI who was walking past and said "I clean your boots, no charge". The GI took him up on his offer and after the kid had polished his boots he started walking off. The kid looked surprised when he never coughed up with any money and ran after the GI shouting "you pay me, you pay me". The Yank took no notice of him and kept on walking. By this time the kid was getting really annoyed as he shouted "everyone here is number one and you number ten", the kid then paused for a second and then shouted " you number ten fuckin' thousand". Everyone around him started laughing except for the Yank, who I'm sure must have wished he'd paid the kid in the first place.

When I received the Xmas parcel from Cheryl I was over the moon and I was even lucky enough to get another parcel from my cousin Janet who sent it all the way from England. Me and Janet corresponded with each other throughout my time in Vietnam.

Most of the other guys also received Xmas parcels. So I think we must have had full stomachs for the first time. I seem to remember being hungry most of the time I was in Vietnam and I think that was the case with most of the other guy's aswell. I recall a day when we were heading back to camp after a patrol and we spotted a cow grazing. It wasn't in a herd, it was totally on its own, and there was no herdsman either. We waited for a while to see if anyone claimed it, but nobody did. So, it was decided one of us should shoot it, cut it up and take it back to camp for the cooks. To be honest I was against the idea and I think some of the other guys were too, but one of the soldiers who said he used to be a butcher in Civvy Street volunteered and he shot it. It was strung up from a tree and some of the guys cut it up with their machetes, and we carried the pieces back to camp. But if my memory serves me right I don't remember getting any extra helpings of meat at meal times. Perhaps the Officers got it all. I'll never know!

When we went out on Operations, I don't think any of us had full stomachs. The Aussie ration packs only contained three small tins of food, one each for breakfast, lunch and dinner. There was also a packet of biscuits that were so hard we used to call them dog biscuits and we also had a bar of chocolate which I think dated back to the First World War.

On rare occasions we were treated to American ration packs. A tin of their food for one meal was the same size as all three Aussie tins put together. They even had fruit cocktail for desert and cigarettes too! Because their ration packs contained so much they were bulky and it meant that you couldn't carry as many day's food as you could with the Aussie ration packs. That's why we only got the American one's occasionally. I think the American Army definitely lives up to the saying "An Army marches on its stomach". I think the Aussie drinks rations took some beating though, when we were in base camp on most day's we'd get issued with two free cans of grog (beer) and two free Goffers (soft drinks). I always swapped my Goffers for Grog with someone.

CHAPTER 13

WOUNDED IN 'NAM

Dear Mam

It's only me again. I thought I'd drop you a line to let you know that I'm okay and to put your mind at rest.

I know the Army have sent you a telegram telling you about me being wounded. I asked them not to send you one but they said with you being the next- of- kin you had to be the first to be notified.

Anyway Mam, believe me it's nothing to worry about at all. I walked into a booby-trap and was hit in the leg by shrapnel. It injured four other guys who were behind me, but we are all doing ok.

The surgeon who operated on me said the shrapnel went into my calf muscle and didn't break any bones, so he reckons it won't take long to heal. I still count myself very lucky as there's a lot of other guys in the ward who are worse off than me. At the moment I'm not sure whether they'll be sending me back to Australia or I'll be staying in Vietnam. However, the Sergeant has told me that I won't be going on anymore Operations or patrols and I'd spend the rest of the time at the base camp. That means I'll be a lot safer and you won't have to worry anymore. It now means I'll be spending New Year in hospital, but when I've got all these lovely American nurses waiting on me hand and foot I don't mind at all.

I'll finish off now Mam because the lights will be going out soon.

Try not to worry,

Your Loving Son, Derek xxxx

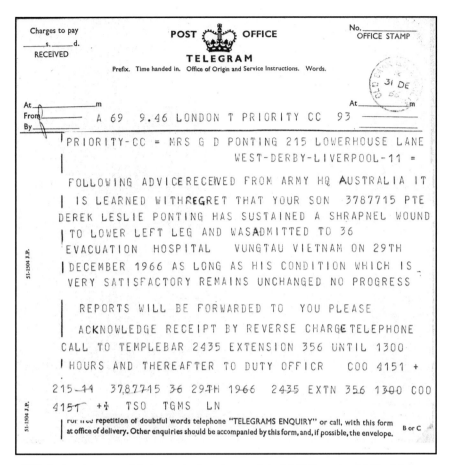

Charges to pay	POST OFFICE	No._____
s.____ d.		OFFICE STAMP
RECEIVED	**TELEGRAM**	
	Prefix. Time handed in. Office of Origin and Service Instructions. Words.	31 DE

At_____m   At_____m
From_____   A 69   9.46 LONDON T PRIORITY CC   93
By_____

PRIORITY-CC = MRS G D PONTING 215 LOWERHOUSE LANE
WEST-DERBY-LIVERPOOL-11 =

FOLLOWING ADVICE RECEIVED FROM ARMY HQ AUSTRALIA IT
IS LEARNED WITH REGRET THAT YOUR SON 3787715 PTE
DEREK LESLIE PONTING HAS SUSTAINED A SHRAPNEL WOUND
TO LOWER LEFT LEG AND WAS ADMITTED TO 36
EVACUATION HOSPITAL   VUNGTAU VIETNAM ON 29TH
DECEMBER 1966 AS LONG AS HIS CONDITION WHICH IS
VERY SATISFACTORY REMAINS UNCHANGED NO PROGRESS

REPORTS WILL BE FORWARDED TO YOU PLEASE
ACKNOWLEDGE RECEIPT BY REVERSE CHARGE TELEPHONE
CALL TO TEMPLEBAR 2435 EXTENSION 356 UNTIL 1300
HOURS AND THEREAFTER TO DUTY OFFICR   COO 4151 +

215-14 3787715 36 29TH 1966 2435 EXTN 356 1300 COO
4151 +1 TSO TGMS LN

For free repetition of doubtful words telephone "TELEGRAMS ENQUIRY" or call, with this form
at office of delivery. Other enquiries should be accompanied by this form, and, if possible, the envelope.   B or C

This is the telegram my Mother received on the morning of 31st December 1966. I believe when she read it, she only got as far as "It is learned with regret that your Son", then she fainted. It must be every parent's nightmare to get a telegram of this type.

Memories...

What I remember of the day I was wounded. It was late afternoon on 29th December 1966, and we'd just returned from a patrol. It was our section's turn to get cleaned up before we had something to eat, so we headed off to a nearby river. I took up the lead position.

Normally the forward Scout would have been Rusty Russell, but on this day fate had him on R&R leave in Hong Kong. Directly behind me was the Corporal and the rest of the section was behind him. As we walked in single file towards the river I had to stop because blocking my way was a stretch of coiled concertina razor wire. I noticed a gap in it where it had been pressed down, which I thought the previous sections had done it when they passed through. I turned to the Corporal and pointed to the gap and he gestured to me to go through. As I did there was a loud bang, and I had no idea what it was. I saw a South Vietnamese soldier (ARVN) running towards us and roaring at us and my first thought was that he must have had something to do with the explosion. But I soon realised that he was in fact warning us of something. At the same time I noticed that some of the guys behind me were lying on the ground. At this point I hadn't realised that I'd been hit myself. As I tried to move my legs, my left leg wouldn't obey me. I looked down and saw blood coming through my trouser leg and I think I fell down on the ground too. I recall seeing Dougie Faint bravely trying to put his field dressing on his stomach were the shrapnel had hit him. I could hear Bill Byers shouting out that he'd lost a finger. The shrapnel had blown it off. The Corporal Roy Pollock was hit in the leg the same as me, but I think the shrapnel had broken a bone in his leg. Dave Hede who was further back in the section received a shrapnel wound to his arm. So all five of us were put out of action and the booby trap had done what it was intended for except fortunately for us it didn't claim any lives.

Everything happened quickly after that. The other soldiers came to our aid straight away. As they approached me, they told me to lie still as I had fallen backwards inside the barbed wire and I was lying in a minefield.

Some of the guys managed to pull me back through the gap in the fence and onto the safe side, they pulled my trousers off to see what injuries I had. Luckily for me the shrapnel had only hit me in the back of the knee and in my calf and everything else appeared to be intact, just! I say just because I think my body had gone into shock and a certain part of my anatomy had shrunk considerably, and at first I thought the worst had happened, but safe to say it hadn't.

Anyway, it didn't take long before the dust-off chopper arrived and we were all taken to an American military hospital in Vung Tau. I remember from the time we were wounded until we arrived at the hospital it was only about 30 minutes. When I was on the operating table I was told to curl up into a foetal position so they could give me an epidural. During the operation as the surgeon removed the shrapnel from my leg I didn't feel any pain whatsoever.

I was lying on my stomach and I was conscious all the time. On the operating table next to me I was watching Dougie Faint who was under a general anaesthetic having the shrapnel removed from his stomach. I believe at one stage he was in a serious condition and it was a 50-50 chance he would pull through. However, I'm glad to say he made a complete recovery. After my operation was over, I was taken to the ward, I had my leg put into a sling and I lay on the bed and fell asleep. Early next morning after the effects of the epidural had worn off, I felt this terrible pain in my leg that woke me up. I told the Nurse and I was given a morphine jab, which worked for a while, but pretty soon the pain was back and I was given another jab of morphine. This went on until in the end I was told I couldn't be given anymore because I'd had more than my quota. But the pain was becoming unbearable and it was probably at this point that I realised that I had a very low pain threshold. I continued to moan and groan for a long time until a male nurse stopped at the foot of my bed and said "Look Soldier, nobody is EVER in that much pain"! And he walked off, His words really hit home and made me think of how much a wimp I was, I managed to bite my lip after that! To make me feel even worse a soldier in the bed opposite had had his foot blown off and there wasn't a sound coming from him.

Anyway, in the end I think we were all happy just to be still alive. But ironically it should not have happened in the first place. Apparently we'd gone in the wrong direction towards the river and we shouldn't have been in that area at all, as it turned out the booby-trap I walked into had been set up by the ARVN and was meant to stop the Viet Cong from attacking our convoys. I was told later that our corporal had been told about this before hand and as a result he lost his stripes. The tripwire that triggered the booby-trap had been cleverly concealed in the fencing which is why I didn't see it, so as my foot caught the wire it pulled the pin out of a hand grenade that was hidden about 10 yds to the left of us, and that's how we were sprayed with shrapnel.

However, catching my foot on the tripwire could have been a blessing in disguise, because if I'd missed it we would have all walked straight into the minefield and we probably wouldn't be here today.

CHAPTER 14

NEW YEAR SPENT IN HOSPITAL

Dear Mam,

I thought I'd let you know how I'm getting on.

I've been in hospital now just on a fortnight and in that time everything has gone really well. My leg is healing very quickly and I've now started walking without my crutches. I've still got a slight limp but the surgeon said once my muscles loosen up I'll be walking normal again. They reckon I'll only be here another 10 days which means I'll have spent just over 3 weeks here altogether.

It looks like I'll be staying in Vietnam because three of the other guys who were wounded with me have been told they're going back to Australia as their injuries are worse than mine. But I believe they'll all make a full recovery.

I'm not really in any hurry to leave hospital because the food is great and you get plenty of it. Also they show the latest movies every night, so you can understand why I'll be sorry to go. I hope the Army telegram didn't spoil your New Year celebrations too much, but at least you knew I was nice and safe in hospital.

Well Mam, I'll sign off now because I think a movie is starting soon. So, look after yourself, give my regards to everyone back home.

Your Loving Son, Derek xxxx

P.S. I forgot to mention, thanks for the lovely Christmas card.

Memories...

I think I made it pretty clear in the letter that I was enjoying myself in hospital and eating well, in fact I put on quite a few pounds while I was there, so it was a bit of a disappointment when I finally had to leave. I didn't have to return to my unit straight away. They sent me to the rest and convalescence centre in VungTau. When I arrived there, I was really surprised to see how nice it was. It was a large private villa with views looking out over the sea, and once again the meals were really nice.

Rest and Convalescence Centre - Vung Tau.

But all things come to an end and after three days I was back in my unit at Nui Dat, after an absence of nearly a month. There were a few new faces in camp. They had come to replace Ray, Bill and Dougie. Me and Dave Hede were the only two who didn't get 'homers'. At one stage I thought I might have got a homer, but I was surprised how quickly my leg healed.

After my operation the surgeon gave me a piece of the shrapnel that he'd taken out of my leg. He said I might want to keep it as a souvenir. It was about the size of a 9mm bullet, so I put it on my bedside cabinet in hospital, but one of the cleaners thinking it a bit of rubbish threw it in the bin, "goodbye souvenir".

Although my leg healed it still wasn't 100% so I think I was expecting some light duties to start with, but the very next day after coming back to camp we were preparing to go out on a search and destroy patrol. I had written to my Mother when I was in hospital that I wouldn't be going out on any more patrols because I wanted her to have peace of mind, so as far as she knew I was staying at base camp for the rest of my time in Vietnam.

Anyway, as we were getting our orders for my first patrol since I walked in to the booby-trap, the Sergeant said "Are there any volunteers for forward scout"? , So I put my hand up and said "Ee ar Sarg", he hesitated for a second, looked straight at me and said "Fuck Off Scouse, from now on you're tail-end Charlie"! He wasn't joking either because from then on I was last man in the section for the remaining time I was in Vietnam. It suited me fine, at least there would be less chance of me walking into another booby-trap! I think the front man was almost always in the most danger, but being at the back also had its dangers too. Although I was last man in the section, it didn't necessarily mean that I had no one behind me. It was only when our section was last in the company that everyone was in front of me and then I was the very last man. I suppose it could get a little scary when that happened. I remember such a time when I was last man and we'd stopped for a shoko. I was that shattered I fell asleep sitting up with my back against a tree. When I woke up, I thought I had been left on my own because I couldn't see any of the other guys. I was just about to start panicking when Dave Hede appeared. He had realised that I wasn't behind him and he came back for me, I hate to think about what might have happened if he hadn't noticed I was missing.

CHAPTER 15

MENTIONED IN THE NEWSPAPERS

Dear Mam,

Thanks for your nice long letter, it always makes me happy when I know you're in good health and looking after yourself.

We've been informed that the five of us who were wounded will each get a Silver Tankard with our name and number on them. If we'd have been in the American Army, we'd have received the Purple Heart medal, I guess we'll have to try and find some way of hanging the tankards on our chest, ha ha!.

I had a letter off Cheryl the other day. She told me you'd sent her the clipping out of the Liverpool Echo about me being wounded. Thanks for that, I'll probably be a hero to her from now on. ha ha!.

One of my mates who's been injured twice since he's been out here and has been mentioned in the Aussie papers each time. The first time he was stung by a swarm of wasps, and the second time he was wounded with me. He reckons all the girls will be after him when he gets home once they've read about him. So, let's hope it's the same for me.

When I was last in Vung Tau, I bought a couple of Vietnamese dolls, one for you and one for Janet. They stand on a small plinth so I think they would look good on the sideboard or mantelpiece. I'll send them off to you as soon as possible. I'll have to close now Mam, so 'til next time. Look after yourself and have a good time,

Your Loving Son Derek xxxx

PS Give my regards to the neighbours.

Memories...

When I came out of hospital and I'd been back with the Company a few weeks, I was given the tankard I was promised. It was silver in colour but made of pewter and inscribed on it was "PTE D.L. PONTING A COY. 6 RAR. WIA VIETNAM 1966-67. I kept it in my trunk while I was in Vietnam, but when I returned to Australia, I used to drink beer from it. When I got back to England, at first I used it as a shaving mug, but after a while I decided to clean it up, and to this day it stands on my bedside cabinet alongside my other Army memorabilia.

The mate I mentioned in the letter who was stung by the wasps and who was wounded with me was Dave Hede. I'm not sure whether his encounter with the wasps was the same as the one I had with them. This particular day we were patrolling through the jungle in a single file when I heard a bit of a commotion coming from the front. The next thing I knew I was told to turn around and start running. I didn't ask any questions I just ran. I didn't know why at that point but I remember thinking aren't we here to fight the enemy not run away from them. It wasn't until later that I found out that the front guys had disturbed a wasp's nest and some of them had multiple stings. Dave might have been one of them.

So, as well as putting up with mosquitoes', leeches and scorpions we now had to add wasps to the list. However, there is another one that I haven't mentioned and it's the one I feared most of all..... the snake! When we first arrived in Vietnam we were told that most, if not all snakes were venomous. Fortunately, I don't recall any of the guys being bitten by any snakes, although in some cases the Viet Cong used to put snakes in the entrances to their underground tunnels.

I remember a day when I had my own experience with a snake. Snakes adapt to whatever type of terrain they are in, and it can therefore be very difficult to spot them. If the foliage was green so were the snakes! If the undergrowth was brown then so were the snakes! The good thing was the snakes couldn't bite through your jungle boots. So it was unlikely that you would be bitten when you were walking along. But my ordeal happened when we stopped for a break and I was sitting down amongst some brown leaves. Suddenly, the leaves started to move towards me and then I realised that the leaves were in fact a brown snake, perfectly camouflaged. I froze and just as it was about to crawl onto my thigh, another soldier who was standing by me had also spotted it and he immediately stamped on it! But that wasn't the end of it because the snake coiled up and then sprang at him, he seemed oblivious to the danger and continued to stamp on the snake until he eventually killed it. I was grateful to the soldier because without his help I don't know what might have happened. I won't mention his name because at the time of the incident I believe that he was drunk and I think that explains why he wasn't scared of the snake. How he managed to get pissed when we were on patrol I'll never know!

All the creatures I've mentioned so far I think you would probably expect to come across in a country like Vietnam, however, there was one I didn't expect to see and especially where it was, and it came as quite a shock to me when I came across one. It happened while we were on an operation. Just before we moved into this particular area the Australian artillery had been bombing it for a few hours and we were told that there was probably a strong contingent of enemy forces there. Once the artillery stopped bombing, we moved in and as we did the first thing I noticed was how quiet everything was, there were no jungle sounds at all, not even the sound of a bird, it was really eerie. I assumed all the bombing had killed or frightened away all the wild life. As we approached a more dense part of the jungle, I spotted it! At first I thought that I was looking at a big log, but as I got closer I couldn't believe my eyes. It was a bloody huge crocodile. It was obviously dead because it was lying on its back and it's stomach was ripped apart, no doubt from the artillery fire. But what I couldn't understand was how it got there, because I couldn't remember being anywhere near water or swamps. I can only assume that the artillery fire had blown the creature a fair old distance. However it seems that artillery wasn't as successful at destroying the Viet Cong. As we carried on through the jungle we came across a large deserted Viet Cong camp site, but there was no damage and no dead Viet Cong!

The Vietnamese dolls I sent to my Mother and cousin Janet were not children's dolls, they were for display. They stood about 12 inches high and were on a wooden plinth. The dolls were dressed in sari type of dress, silk pantaloons and conicle hat. Lots of the other guys sent these dolls home too. My Mother took my advice and put the doll on the sideboard and when I returned home it was still there.

LIVERPOOL MAN HURT IN VIETNAM

A 21-years-old Liverpool soldier, Private Derek Leslie Ponting, has been wounded while fighting in Vietnam with the Australian Army.

Private Ponting, whose parents live at 215 Lowerhouse Lane, West Derby, was injured in the leg by shrapnel when a Vietcong booby trap exploded near him.

Derek, who emigrated to Australia two years ago with a cousin, was called up for the fighting in Vietnam over a year ago. His mother said to-day that she had received a telegram to say that his condition in hospital was satisfactory.

Derek, whose interests are judo and boxing, is a former pupil of Stonebridge Lane Secondary School and before leaving for Australia was a van driver for a Liverpool laundry.

Pte Ponting

ENGLISHMAN IS WOUNDED IN VIETNAM

CANBERRA. — A young Englishman, serving as a National Serviceman with the 6th Battalion, Royal Australian Regiment, has been wounded in Vietnam.

He is Pte. **Derek Leslie Ponting**, 21, single, of West Derby, Liverpool, England.

Pte. Ponting was on patrol with four Australians near the task force base in Phuoc Tuy province last week, when an exploding Viet Cong booby trap injured all five.

Pte. Ponting was evacuated to a field hospital at Vung Tau with shrapnel wounds to the lower left leg. His condition is satisfactory.

Briton wounded

CANBERRA: Derek Leslie Ponting, 21, an English immigrant conscripted into the Australian Army, is in hospital with shrapnel wounds after he and four Australians were caught in a Vietcong booby trap.

CHAPTER 16

LOST COMRADES

Dear Mam,

Thanks very much for your letter I'm glad you got your birthday card okay. I'm sorry I couldn't get you a better one, but they don't have much of a selection out here. Still, it's the thought that counts, isn't it?

I don't know if you heard in the papers back home about the terrible accident that happened here the other day. Delta Company were out on patrol and the New Zealand artillery who are attached to us, fired on their position thinking they were the enemy. I don't know how that was possible but they killed four of our soldiers and wounded about 12. I knew two of those who died and they were real nice guys. It's very upsetting but you've got to carry on and hope those who were wounded pull through.

I'm due for a few days leave soon in Vung Tau so I'll have time to reflect on things. I met up with a couple of mates last week who I was with in 7 RAR. They've been in Vietnam for a while but it's the first chance we've had to get together. We had a few drinks and talked about the good times we had back in Australia.

I'll sign off now Mam, so 'til next time, Look after yourself

Your Loving Son,

Derek xxxx

Memories...

I remember the day really well when Delta Company was bombed by
the New Zealand artillery. It came as a great shock to us all. Four
Australian soldiers were killed and eleven wounded some seriously.
It would seem that Delta Company have had more than their share
of bad luck. They also suffered the most fatalities during the Battle
of Long Tan. In the letter to my Mother I mentioned that I knew
two of the soldiers that had been killed. They were Jack Kirby and
Dougie Powter. Jack was the CSM of Delta Company and I reported
to him when I left 1 ARU and joined his company.

It states on the Vietnam Veterans nominal roll that I joined Alpha
Company from 1 ARU, however I remember spending about a week
or two in Delta Company before I joined Alpha Company. I can't
remember why that happened, but in the short time I was there I
found CSM Kirby a fair and approachable man. He was a big man
in stature and he was very well respected by his fellow soldiers. He
was also a hero. During the Battle of Long Tan he was awarded the
Distinguished Conduct Medal for his bravery. It seems a tragedy
that he should survive such a battle against the North Vietnamese
Army only to be killed by so called "friendly fire".

The other soldier who I knew that had died was Dougie Powter.
I first met Dougie at the Reinforcement Centre in Ingleburn and
when we were in Vietnam we were at 1 ARU at the same time. Later
we went to Delta Company and that's when fate played its part, as
I left for Alpha Company and he stayed with Delta. Dougie was
evacuated to hospital but died later of his wounds. I remember we
were all praying for him to pull through, but sadly it wasn't to be. We
lost a really nice guy.

It's always hard to take when you lose a comrade and even harder
when it comes from friendly fire, because you know it should never
have happened. Fortunately I don't think there were many occasions
involving friendly fire with the Australian forces. However, I recall

a time when I was with Alpha Company when we had a narrow escape. We had come into contact with the enemy and we called in for support from our mortars. Somehow they got the grid reference wrong and the bombs fell short and practically landed right on top of us. All we could do was hit the deck and hope for the best. Our radio operator managed to get through and divert them away from us and miraculously no one was hurt, but it could have so easily been another tragic incident. Jack Kirby's Distinguished Conduct Medal was just one example of the many awards received for bravery during the Vietnam War. During the war four Australians were awarded the Victoria Cross, which is the highest honour that can be awarded in battle. During my time in Vietnam I heard about numerous brave acts, one man's name in particular was often mentioned for his leadership and bravery. His name is Sergeant Frank Alcorta from Alpha Company and all soldiers and officers held him in the highest regard. It seems amazing he only received "Mentioned in Dispatches" (MID) award. Many of us thought it was a travesty because we believed that he deserved much higher recognition. I recall one Operation when I witnessed firsthand his leadership and bravery. We came into contact with company size strength of Viet Cong and they opened fire on us. The bullets started flying through the foliage and me and Dave Hede dived behind this mound of earth for cover. But not Sergeant Alcorta who was still standing and with complete disregard for his own safety he was shouting at us to get off our stomachs and do a sweep towards the enemy. We obeyed his orders and got up and with the help of our mortars we were able to overrun the enemy position. I don't know what the casualty figures were that day but I saw at least one dead Viet Cong. I heard of other acts of Sergeant Alcorta's bravery and in Lt Col Mollison's book "Long Tan and Beyond" he also states that he deserved greater recognition.

It was great meeting up with a couple of mates who I'd last seen in Puckapunyal. They were two of my closest friends from 7 RAR, Kevin Leder and Lloyd Anstey. I knew it wouldn't be long after I'd left Puckapunyal and Ingleburn that they'd joined me in Vietnam.

However they were both posted to different companies which meant our reunion was only a brief one. We did manage to have a few drinks together and talk about the laughs we used to have back in Australia. Unfortunately, it was to be the last time the three of us would be reunited. However, I do know that they both survived the war and returned safely back Australia.

Although I was a Rifleman and my job was to go out on 'search and destroy' patrols sometimes someone would have to stay behind in the camp at Nui Dat to do certain jobs. One of these jobs was to clean the latrines! Apart from it being a very unpleasant job I also felt that it was very demeaning. It was a job for one person and you had to do it for a whole week. They used to ask for a volunteer but there were never any takers. On this particular day the Sergeant asked for a volunteer for the "Blowfly job", called this for obvious reasons, as usual nobody offered to do it and you've guessed it, he picked me. The only plus side to the job was it only took about three hours each day and you didn't go on any patrols so the rest of the day could be spent relaxing.

There were lots of guys using these latrines so you can imagine that I had plenty of flies to contend with. The latrines where situated in wooden sheds and they had deep pits dug into them. The pits were like a long trench and they were probably about 10 feet deep. There was a wooden structure above the trench with holes in it where you sat to do your business. Of course there was no privacy, but if you'll pardon the pun... nobody gave a shite anyway. After I finished my week as Blowfly it was someone else's turn. Again nobody volunteered, but I was shocked when the Sergeant said to me "you did such a good job last week Scouse, so you can have another go"! So I ended up doing a week longer than anyone else. A few of the guys used to take the piss out of me after that, if anyone shouted "have you seen Scouse", someone would say "Oh you mean Blowfly". On the subject of latrines, our Logistics camp in Vung Tau was a little bit more up market, you had the luxury of your own cubicle, no doors on them but a degree of privacy, and you could actually sit on a proper toilet bowl and seat, it had a flush too! The local Vietnamese cleaned them each day.

I remember one day I was sitting on the loo in VungTau and I heard the cleaner mopping around the other cubicles. I thought when he gets to me he'll just go past and onto the next cubicle. But to my surprise and embarrassment he, turned out to be a she, gave me a big smile, mopped around my feet and moved on into the next cubicle! But that's the way it was in Vietnam, the women didn't seem to be embarrassed about things like that. You would often see them squatting down for a pee in the paddy fields, but to be fair there was nowhere else for them to go.

***

There was another job I was assigned to do in Nui Dat and that was to work on the switchboard. It was situated partially underground and covered in sandbags, this made it quite safe from any bombings. It was quite claustrophobic inside as there was only just enough room for one person to sit comfortably behind the switchboard. Anyway the Sergeant told me that I was to take incoming calls for a few hours. He explained to me that I had to put the plug in the hole when a red light showed up and then speak into the mouthpiece, what could be more simple than that, I thought. Anyway with the cramped conditions I managed to position my chair so that I could stretch my legs out and rest them on the corner of the switchboard. After about half an hour had passed and no red lights had come on, I thought to myself, what a cushy job this is, I hope they ask me to do this again. Another half hour went by and still no red lights appeared but by this time I was getting bored. Then all of a sudden the Sergeant burst in through the door and shouted "what the fuckin hell is going on, get your fuckin feet off the switchboard", he said. As soon as I took my feet off he leaned over and flicked a switch on, I must have accidentally knocked it off with my foot. The whole switchboard lit up like a Christmas tree! The Sergeant called me a dickhead and told me to piss off to my tent. Needless to say I was never asked back to work on the switchboard again!

CHAPTER 17

VUNG TAU EXPERIENCES

In many of the letters that I sent my Mother I often mentioned Vung Tau. The Australians had their main logistics camp there. It was situated on the beach and it was only a small distance from Vung Tau town centre. We spent our R & C leave there, and some of us also had our R & R leave there. Sometimes if we had been on a long operation we would be rewarded with a few days off to chill out there. The following are some of my experiences of my visits to Vung Tau.

On my first visit to Vung Tau I still hadn't had my dentures replaced since I lost them in the river crossing at Canungra. I hadn't seen the point as who is going to take any notice of you in Vietnam? However a couple of embarrassing moments proved me wrong! When some kids saw the gap in my teeth they started laughing at me, and another time some bar girls thought it was funny too. I noticed that all the young Vietnamese seemed to have nice white teeth, but it was a different story for the older ones. A lot of them used to suck what looked like a large gobstopper, it was called Beetle Nut. When they sucked it their mouths turned red, eventually their teeth went permanently jet black... not a pretty sight!

Anyway eventually I went to see the Army dentist back at camp and was lucky to be fitted with a new set of dentures. I don't think they were the best fit in the world, at times I felt like I was breaking them in for Red Rum, but they gave me more confidence for my future visits to Vung Tau.

***

On the street corners in Vung Tau you would often see Vietnamese guys selling cigarettes and other things. As you walked passed them they would say "You want to buy Fuck pictures?" These were pornographic photos and funnily enough some of the girls in these photos were the same girls that served us in the shops and bars. You used to get some of the soldiers pointing to the photos and saying to them "Is this you?" and they always replied "No, no not me", but we always knew it was them.

The Yanks used to spend their R & C leave in Vung Tau too, and we would often mingle with them in the bars. I remember a time when I was with three mates and we got talking to an American sailor. I think he was a chief petty officer and he invited us back to his ship. None of us had been on an American warship before, and we gladly accepted as we thought it would make a change from drinking in the bars all the time. We made arrangements to meet him at the harbour the next day. His ship was anchored a short distance out at sea, so we boarded a landing craft to set off for the ship. The landing craft were the same that you see in the movies, the type that land on beaches and then the flat front drops down. By the time we got to the ship we were soaked to the skin with the waves crashing over the top, I promised myself if I was ever in one again I would definitely make sure I wore waterproofs!

Once on board we were introduced to some of the crew who seemed really surprised to see four Aussies on their patch, but just the same they gave us a warm welcome. After a tour of the ship, which was really interesting we were taken to the mess, by this time we were spitting feathers. What would you lads like to drink said the Yank, we all came back with the same answer " a beer thanks Mate", he gave a little laugh and we looked at each other, what's funny we thought, "No" he said "I mean would you like a cup of tea, coffee or a Goffer (soft drink). Sorry guys, but we don't have alcohol on any of our ships." After we got over the shock we drank our Goffers and we couldn't get back to Terra Firma quick enough and get back to some real drinking!

The stress of being on patrol and being in the jungle for months on end meant that when we were let loose in Vung Tau we made the most of it. More often than not that meant we had too much alcohol. I remember once I got into trouble, I was drinking in this bar with my mates and it was getting late. I went to the toilet and when I came out to my surprise my mates had gone. They must have been drunk too and never realised they had left me behind! It then dawned on me that it was only a few minutes to curfew and it would take me at least 10 minutes in a taxi to get back to camp. Anyway, I thought I'd take a chance trying to get back so I went outside and flagged down this scooter taxi. I jumped onto the back and told him to get me to the camp pronto! So off he sped, but as we were going through town the curfew had started. To ensure that people kept to the curfew the Vietnamese police used to patrol the bars and surrounding area. The Aussies nicknamed the Vietnamese police the White Mice, most of them were only about five foot nothing, and with me standing all of five foot six inches in my stocking feet, it's the first time I've literally looked down on a policeman!! They were dressed all in white, cap, shirt and trousers, hence the white mice tag. Anyway, there I was travelling pillion on this scooter when we passed one of the white mice and he started to blow his whistle. The scooter driver slammed his breaks on as hard as he could and I nearly ended up over the handlebars! As I turned around the policeman had pulled his gun from his holster and was pointing it straight at us. I remember thinking later, what would have happened if the driver hadn't stopped, would he have fired at the tyres or shot me in the back! Thankfully it never came to that. He came over to us and shouted at the driver and then sent him on his way. He then turned to me and said "You go" and pointed across the road to the nearest building, it was obvious he wanted me off the street as soon as possible. The building he pointed me towards was a right dump, and as drunk as I was I realised that I had no choice so I walked over and went inside. It was some sort of hotel come dosshouse. I paid for a room, if you could call it that, to be more precise I paid for a bed! The bed was situated down a long corridor, there were other beds opposite and a curtain you could pull across if you wanted privacy and that was it. I paid for a girl to spend the night with me, and that turned out to be another mistake! What a night! Behind the curtains in the other "rooms" more soldiers had girls with them too. But what I found strange was that I couldn't hear any Aussies, all the soldiers where Yanks and they were all Black G.I's. Anyway, during the early hours I asked the girl where the toilet was, she pointed down the corridor so I jumped off the bed, in my nuddy and landed ankle deep in water. The heavy rain during the night had flooded the place. On the way back from the toilet, wading through the water, some Yank was leaning over his bed and pissing into the water. He was either too drunk, too lazy or just didn't want to get his feet wet, but I don't think he was the only one doing it because before too long the place stunk to high heaven! I couldn't wait for the curfew to end so I could get back to camp as quick as possible. However, my ordeal wasn't over yet! When I woke up in the morning the girl had left, nothing unusual about that I thought until I started to get dressed and couldn't find my boots. Now the Aussie boots were a prized possession for the Vietcong if they could get hold of them. They are made of leather and I believe they had a sheet of steel through the sole which helped protect you from Punji traps.

My boots were only size seven (42) which probably meant they would fit most of the Vietnamese guys. But there were lots of big Aussies in our Battalion so I don't think their boots would have been much good to the tiny Viet Congs. I just couldn't imagine them running through the jungle in size 12 boots!

I had heard of a tale of an Aussie soldier who was lying seriously wounded after a battle when he felt someone tugging at his feet. He looked down and to his horror, a Viet Cong, thinking that the Aussie was dead was taking his boots off. The Aussie sat up suddenly and shouted FUCK OFF! The Viet Cong got such a shock he turned and ran off! So, you can understand my concern when at first I couldn't find my boots. It wasn't just my boots that was missing, when I took them off I put all my money into them! I can't remember how much I had but it was a hell of a lot of money because it was my first day on leave. I searched around and then to my relief I found my boots underneath her pillow, what a relief. I put my hand inside them and you've guessed it.... all my money was gone! I went looking for the girl but she was nowhere to be seen. I confronted the Momma San and told her the girl had stolen my money and I asked where she lived. She told me in broken English that the girl had left that morning and gone to see her Momma and Poppa in Saigon. I thought oh well at least I've contributed to a family reunion and it's yet another case of live and learn!

When I eventually got back to camp I told the guys where the brothel was and described to them exactly the area it was in. They all fell about laughing and said "you Dickhead Scouse, everyone knows that place is nicknamed Pox Alley". So, as a result and as the name implies, for my troubles I got the VC - no not the Victoria Cross – the Vietnamese Clap!

I remember another story from Vung Tau which I thought was quite funny but didn't directly involve me. As most of us were young single guys, obviously whenever we were on leave, at the top of the agenda was always beer and sex.

I recall this day when there were about six of us having a drink in a bar. One guy was on his first leave in Vung Tau, he was a "Nasho" like myself. I won't mention his name to save him any embarrassment, so I'll just refer to him as Jim. Anyway Jim wanted to know where he could get his "leg-over". We told him there was a place nearby, it was a Barber shop that doubled as a sex shop! Jim asked us to go with him, but we were all more interested in having a few beers and getting pissed. He seemed a shy and naive guy and some of us thought he might even be a "cherry boy" (virgin). He asked us what he should say when he got in the shop and we told him not to have intercourse just in case he got a dose (VD). So we told him to ask for a Suck Fuck, which in today's vocabulary is a blow-job! But I don't think it would have been wise to ask for a blow-job in a Barber's because I think you'd get something totally different than what you wanted! So Jim went to the Barbers and no sooner had he gone than he was back again, looking very red faced. We said "that's

97

got to be the quickest sex session on record?" Jim said "I didn't have any sex I was too embarrassed", " why what happened" we said, He told us that when he walked into the Barber's there were quite a few people sitting down waiting to get their hair cut and one of them was an Australian Army officer. Jim went over to the Momma San and spoke in a soft voice so nobody could hear him "I want to pay for a Suck Fuck", she didn't hear what he said so he repeated it a little louder, still making sure nobody heard him. This time she realised what he said and at the top of her voice shouted "AH, YOU WANT A SUCK FUCK" with that everyone turned and looked at him, so he did a quick about turn and walked out, we all fell about laughing.

I remember an embarrassing time I once had in Vung Tau which took place in a massage parlour. When I came out of the sauna I was lying on the table with only a towel round my middle. A young Vietnamese girl walked through the curtains, she looked about 18 years old, and she was very pretty and had a nice figure too. She started to give me a massage, cracking all my bones. She even stood on my back and cracked my shoulder blades with her feet. Then she told me to lie on my back and as I did my towel slipped to the floor and she could see that I was aroused. Do you want "bum-bum" (intercourse) she said, I nodded, closed my eyes for a few seconds and when I opened them she was gone!

That's when I got the shock of my life, in walked another girl, stark naked and resembling a sumo wrestler, but not as good looking! She even had pot marks on her cheeks! Before I could do anything she jumped on top of me and pinned me to the table! At that moment I realised I had two options, fight her or have sex with her, and considering that she weighed about 40lbs more than me, reluctantly I chose the latter!

CHAPTER 18

ANOTHER TRAGEDY

Dear Mam

With this letter I've also sent a tape recording. I hope you enjoy hearing my voice again after all this time. The tape recorder we used wasn't in the best condition, but I still hope you manage to make out everything that's said on it.

Well Mam, I'm afraid I've got more bad news to report. This time it's from our own company that a soldier has been killed. We were returning back to camp in the early hours of the morning when he stood on a mine and was killed instantly. So you can imagine we are all feeling pretty down at the moment. It happened only a short distance in front of me. I know I told you I wasn't going out on any more patrols, but I only said that to stop you worrying about me however, this time I'm telling the truth when I say that Alpha Company are moving to a secure location in Dat Do, called the Horseshoe. It's supposed to be one of the safest areas in Vietnam. Our main task is to build bunkers and erect barbwire fences around the area, so that it's ready in time for the next battalion.

We've been told that we'll be staying there until the end of our tour, which should be sometime in June. I've enclosed some photos I've had taken over the past few weeks. The one of me that looks like I'm in quicksand and covered in mud was taken on Operation Portsea and it was also my birthday.

Well Mam, that's all for now so look after yourself and keep smiling

Your loving Son
Derek xxxx

Note: In this and the previous letter some of the incidents I've mentioned took place 6 weeks apart, so it would seem that some of my letters went astray, unless it was a period when for whatever reason we didn't correspond, I'm not really sure.

Memories...

The day we lost one of our own from Alpha Company was a very sad day for all of us. John Ashton was the only soldier from Alpha Company to be killed during the whole 12 months tour of duty in Vietnam. John was a National Serviceman and he could speak Vietnamese. He was a great loss to the Company and also the battalion. I was there when he was killed and I will always remember it.

The day before he died we were preparing to go on an all-night ambush. We'd been told that the Viet Cong were known to be using a certain area during the night. Alpha Company were sent to that area to set up ambush positions. As night time approached we took up our positions and everything was going to plan. All that was needed was for the enemy to appear. A few hours went by with no sign of anyone, more hours passed and still nothing. By this time we were finding it hard to keep our eyes open. Then we began to feel water coming up through the ground beneath us, we had no idea where it was coming from because it hadn't even been raining. We had to find higher ground quickly and some of us even climbed up into the trees. It was an uncomfortable night for all of us and all in vain because we never made contact with the enemy throughout.

At first light we were all exhausted after being awake for so long. As we headed back to camp, we walked down a dirt road in single file sections on each side of the road. We had only been going along the road for about 5 minutes when it happened!

I heard the sound of a loud explosion about 20 yards in front of me. The first thing I thought was we'd made contact with the enemy, but it soon got down the line back to us what had happened. John had stood on a mine as he walked across the road to speak to another soldier Mick Sweeney, who was also seriously wounded in the explosion. John, I believe, died immediately. His body was carefully wrapped in tarpaulin and placed in an armoured personnel carrier (APC). Me and a few other soldiers climbed into the back of the APC with John and we headed off back to camp. The journey to camp took about 10 minutes and during that time hardly a word was spoken, we were all in deep thought. I don't know what the other guys were thinking but as I was looking down at his body lying at my feet my first thought was of his Mother. Although I didn't know his family I knew that the news of her son's death would turn her life upside down and it would never be the same again. At the same time I was thinking what if it had been me who had died? How would my Mother and family have reacted? And with that in mind, strangely, it gave me some comfort. When we arrived back at camp the CSM was waiting for us with some consoling words.

Mines and booby traps were always a worry in Vietnam. The Australians lost over 120 servicemen in this way, and many more were wounded. It's the same today in Iraq and Afghanistan. It saddens me so much when I see on TV the pictures of our soldiers coming home in coffins and others with horrific injuries caused by landmines. When I was in Vietnam I heard a story about a young Australian who lost both his legs in a landmine explosion. I believe that he had been a very good footballer before he went into the Army. I don't know how true it was but I was told that Douglas Bader was asked to fly out and offer him some moral support. Douglas Bader of course was the World War Two hero who lost both his legs in a flying accident. He was a great all round sportsman before his injuries, and he became a legend in his own lifetime. I hope that they did meet and that it helped in his rehabilitation.

I know I was lucky when I nearly walked into the minefield, but I had also had an encounter with a mine before that! It happened when we were guarding the engineers who were preparing an area for a landing strip. We were walking in single file on each side of a bulldozer when all of a sudden there was a loud explosion. The front part of the bulldozer, the bit that scoops up the dirt, had hit a mine and it took the full blast so thankfully nobody was hurt. Of course if someone had stood on the mine it would have been a totally different story. After that happened I was walking with a lot more caution and I was trying to tread into the same footsteps as the soldier who was in front of me. A lot of soldiers believed in fate, and on many occasions you would hear them saying "When your number's up, it's up!" However, I know of a couple of incidents were the guys would have thought that their number was definitely up only to escape within an inch of their lives by sheer luck!

Nigel Snashall from Alpha Company was one such lucky person. One day we came under attack and as Nigel was returning fire, an enemy bullet made a direct hit to the front part of the wooden stock which goes round the barrel of his rifle. Splinters flew up into his face but otherwise he was unhurt, one millimetre either way and he wouldn't be alive today. I also heard of another incident which involved a claymore mine, which I think is an American invention.

The Viet Cong would sometimes get hold of one of these mines. When these mines were detonated they would spray dozens of ball bearings in an arched area to give maximum effect. Another one of our soldiers was caught up in such a blast but amazingly he escaped unhurt even though a ball bearing went right through his bush hat. A fraction lower and it would have been in his head!

Lucky escape. A soldier puts his finger through a hole in his bush hat while his mate examines his head.

102

During our time in Vietnam we often had Kiwis (New Zealanders) attached to us and on the odd occasion we would go on patrol with the Americans. We also worked alongside the South Vietnamese Army or to give them their correct name as it was then the Army Republic of Vietnam (ARVN). When I first set eyes on them they didn't impress me very much. I'm not saying they weren't experienced fighting men, but somehow I felt that they were lacking in discipline and seemed very laid back. You would see them strolling along with their rifles across their shoulders and quite often they would be seen in pairs holding hands!

To me, I don't think that gives the image of a tough fighting soldier. However, I was reliably informed that they were not gay, it was their way of showing their friendship towards each other.

Laid back Arvn Troops on guard outside officers quarters in Vung Tau.

103

We had an ARVN soldier attached to us in Alpha Company, he was also our interpreter, but I can assure you that he never tried to hold hands with any of us! His name with Dingy Dung, I don't know if that is the right spelling but we just called him Dung for short and no we didn't nickname him Shitty arse either! He was about the same age as us Nasho's and I thought he was a nice guy. Apparently, he was born in North Vietnam but for whatever reason he ended up fighting for the South. He accompanied us on all our operations and accounted for himself each time.

I often wonder what happened to him after the war ended. Did he escape to America or Australia? Or was he left to the mercy of the invading North Vietnamese Army. I just hope everything turned out okay for him

Dingy Dung. A South Vietnamese soldier attached to us at Alpha Company as an interpreter.

In some of the letters that I sent home to my Mother I used to include a few photographs. One that I had taken on Operation Portsea, it looks like I've got a smile on my face, but I don't remember why. It was taken on my 22nd Birthday and you can see the muddy conditions that we had to put up with

Operation Porsea.
Picture taken on my 22nd birthday.

I think that it was on this operation that I got into a bit of trouble. It happened when we had to cross a river that had become swollen with all the rain. Small boats were used to cross the river to get to the other side, but the problem was that the riverbank was very muddy. When it was my turn to get into the boat I put my rifle in first and then attempted to jump in, but I got stuck in the mud up to my ankles and the boat drifted off without me, and with it went my rifle! Just then the Sergeant came over and said "where's your fuckin' rifle"? I told him it was on the other side of the river and that I was stuck, but it still didn't stop him from giving me a bollocking for not having my rifle with me. Anyway, the boat came back for me and the guys pulled me out of the mud and I was reunited with my rifle! I hate to think what would have happened if we had come into contact with the enemy while I was stuck in the mud! I still had my hand grenades, but there was no doubt that I was a sitting duck! However, not all our operations were in muddy conditions. Sometimes we had to contend with the bamboo terrain which in my opinion was more frustrating than the mud. You would constantly get snagged by the sharp thorns and you'd end up with your Greens (clothes) ripped and your face and hands scratched to ribbons. After struggling through it for a while I used to get quite annoyed with myself and instead of releasing the thorns with my hands I would just drag myself through it. But I remember getting a fright one time when I realised I couldn't move. At first I thought that it was my webbing that was caught up in the bamboo, but when I looked down to my horror I could see that a thorn was inside the ring pull of my hand grenade. I'm not saying it would have pulled the pin out, because they are spliced wide apart and need a really good tug to pull the pin out, but all the same it made me a lot more cautious after that. It has been known that some soldiers have been killed by their own grenades.

*Thirsty work
amongst the bamboo.*

*Me outside my tent
in Nui Dat.*

Me in rubber plantation with SLR Rifle.

Me returning from a patrol. Note field dressing on butt of rifle.

Me on patrol through the bamboo once again.

Me and Dave Hede with experimental mosquito hats. I think we look more like bee keepers!

Me enjoying a can of beer on the beach at Vung Tau.

Me and Peter Hensell in rubber plantation at Nui Dat. Our tents in the background.

Living quarters at Nui Dat, 1967.

Huey Helicopter used in operations.

Typical market in Vung Tau, 1967.

Old man salutes as patrol goes past.

CHAPTER 19

7 RAR ARRIVE IN VIETNAM

Dear Mam,

Thanks for your lovely letter. I'm glad you received the tape recording okay, and that you liked it so much. It sounded as though it caused quite a bit of excitement when it arrived. By that, I mean you tripping over your dressing gown as you rushed down the stairs when the postman delivered it. And also our Brian leaving for work late so that he could listen to it first. Anyway Mam let's hope the next time you hear my voice it will be in person. I think I've got about a month left to serve in Vietnam and I'm counting the days off one by one. My next letter might be the last one from here.

I've heard my old battalion 7 RAR are now in Vietnam and are soon to take over from us. They went on their first operation the other day and had some success. They made contact with the enemy and the good news is that none of our lads were injured. They've also brought tracker dogs with them from Australia and they're already proving very useful. The dogs followed some blood trails after a contact which led them to a couple of wounded Viet Cong.

As I told you we're now at the Horseshoe in Dat Do, but we've still got some way to go before we finish the barbwire fencing and bunkers. It's hard work but we still get more time to relax than we did before we came here. I've even learnt to play chess in my spare time. I mentioned in my last letter that the Horseshoe is one of the safest places in Vietnam. One of the reasons being we are surrounded by our own minefields. But two Americans who were attached to us, for some unknown reason walked into the minefield and were killed.

I received a letter off Cheryl the other day, but it wasn't the type I usually get from her because it was a Dear John letter. She told me she had met someone she really likes.

I suppose it's for the best really because I was always going to come home when I got out of the Army. Besides there was never any plans to get married or engaged. Anyway good luck to her, I hope she'll be happy.

Well Mam, that's about all I can think of for now, so I'll finish off.

Look after yourself, write soon

Your loving son
Derek xxxx

Memories...

I remember sending my Mother the tape recording of my voice, but I have no idea what I said on it. I borrowed it off one of my mates who'd brought it with him from Australia. It was a big old bulky thing which had two large spools on top and it had definitely seen better days. However the main thing was that it worked even though the tapes sounded crackly. Although I can't remember what I said on the tape I remember the sounds that were going on in the background. You could hear choppers constantly flying overhead and the sound of the artillery guns going off all the time. In the letters I sent my Mother I used to try to play down the dangers to her so she wouldn't worry too much. But, looking back I suppose the sounds in the background might have made her think otherwise. However, when I received a letter from her there was no mention of her being worried, she was just happy to hear my voice after such a long time. She obviously knew about the dangers but she just had to accept them.

***

With my old battalion arriving in Vietnam it meant that our tour of duty in Vietnam was drawing to an end.

7 RAR brought tracker dogs with them from Australia and I think that was the first time the Aussies had used them in Vietnam. I'm sure if 6 Battalion had used them I would have known about it and I would have volunteered to be one of their handlers because I have always loved dogs. I suppose to some people it may seem cruel to use dogs in this way but I believe that the dogs really enjoyed the job. Of course there is always the danger element, but if they saved soldier's lives and warn them of dangers then they are well worth it. Even today tracker dogs are used in Iraq and Afghanistan and are still proving to be very successful.

So, as I mentioned in my letter we moved from our camp in Nui Dat to the Horseshoe at Dat Do, which I told my Mother was a much safer place. Of course we still had to go on patrols but once again I kept that information from my Mother. What I meant by a much safer place was that we where situated in a large hilly area that was shaped like a horseshoe, hence its adopted name. The position of the camp meant that you could see clearly for miles around and it would make it very difficult for the enemy to attack us. We had built bunkers all around the area, some of them had 50 calibre machine guns. We also had barbwire fencing and minefields surrounding us and with thousand of sandbags that had been filled you could say we were well prepared for any type of attack. However, there were still fatalities. We had an American artillery unit attached to us and one day a tragic accident happened which involved two of their soldiers. This particular day I heard a loud explosion and at first I thought we were under attack, but news soon reached us what had in fact happened. Apparently, two American soldiers had been filling sandbags to put around their artillery gun. One of the soldiers spotted a sandbag that had already been filled and went to fetch it. Unfortunately, it was on the other side of the barbwire fencing and that area was heavily mined. How they didn't know it was the minefield we will never know, it was unbelievable and baffling! At first I thought that both soldiers had been killed, as I mentioned in the letter to my Mother. However, I found out later that the guy who had walked into the minefield had his leg blown off, and survived. The other soldier who stayed on the safe side of the fence was hit by shrapnel from the blast and he was killed. One of our own soldiers Private David Buckwalter was first one the scene and he bravely walked into the minefield and administered first aid to the wounded soldier which probably saved his life. Private David Buckwalter was rewarded for his bravery by being mentioned in dispatches (MID). Three Australian soldiers were also killed on the Horseshoe during my time there. Again two soldiers were accidently killed by our own mines and the other soldier I believe accidently shot himself.

We seemed to have more time to relax at the Horseshoe and I don't think we went on as many patrols as we did before. Our ration packs were a lot better too. When we weren't out on patrol we were issued with larger ration packs, they were meant for about 5 persons! Most of the time we would put all the contents of the tins into one pot and make a type of stew. One day someone suggested putting some curry powder in it to add some flavour. I was dead against the idea because I didn't like curry. I remember back at home my Dad used to make himself a curry every week, and I couldn't stand the smell of it. Anyway, it was put to the vote and I was the only one to vote against the curry so in it went! That meant that I had to eat it or go hungry. Needless to say I got stuck in and to my great surprise I enjoyed every mouthful and to this day there isn't a week that goes by when I don't have a curry, whether it's a Chinese one, Indian takeaway and also homemade. While I am on the subject of food I'd like to mention our cooks in Nui Dat, who under very difficult conditions always prepared really nice meals for us, although we could have done with bigger portions.

When I received the Dear John letter from Cheryl, it came as a bit of a shock to me because in her previous letters there had been no hint that anything was wrong between us. But looking back I suppose that it was the right thing for her to do. I think that I should have treated her better because when I was on leave, most of the time I was with the lads and we never got to spend much time on our own. So when I got the letter I understood why she made the decision to be with someone else, some of the other guys also got Dear John letters so I wasn't on my own.

When I returned to Australia I still made a point of meeting up with Cheryl to see if she still felt the same way or if she had changed her mind. So when we met up we kissed and hugged we had a good talk. But after a while it was obvious that she hadn't changed her mind about us and she was in love with someone else. However, it didn't stop us from going to the movies that night and even to this day I can remember the film that we went to see.... it was Georgie Girl. It's funny how some things stick in your mind isn't it? Anyway after the film ended I took her home and we might have shed a tear or two but we parted amicably and I never saw her again. It wasn't that long afterwards that I heard that she was married and then later heard that she had a baby boy. I will always remember that Christmas parcel that she sent to me while I was in Vietnam and especially with the words she wrote "To the best fella in the world, Merry Christmas"

CHAPTER 20

TIME TO REFLECT

Dear Mam,

Thanks very much for your nice long letter which I have just received. It's good to know everyone at home is well. I am doing okay too. You asked me how my leg was shaping up. Well it's not completely back to normal. It still aches now and again but the good news is I no longer have a limp.

I'm glad to hear the weather at home is getting a lot warmer. It's still hot here as usual. I wonder how I'll cope with the cold weather when I get back to England. I should be home by late November, so I don't expect it to be warm. After being used to the hot climates in Vietnam and Australia I'll probably feel the cold even more.

Well Mam it's not long now before we leave Vietnam and of course everyone is looking forward to going home. Most of the guys from 6 Battalion will have been here for 12 months which is a long time to be away from family and friends. I've only been here 8 months and even that seems a long time. However, the other guys are lucky in one respect as they'll be back home in Australia while I'll have to wait another 6 months before I'm back home in England. Anyway as long as we get back safely, that's the main thing.
I'm really pleased to know you've had the spare bedroom decorated for when I get home, thanks for that.

I'm sorry I can't make this letter as long as yours Mam, but I've ran out of things to say at the moment, so 'til next time,

Look after yourself and have a good time
Your loving Son

Derek xxxx

Memories...

My Mother must have still been a bit concerned about my leg as she asked how it was. I reassured her that it was okay apart from aching now and then.

It's now 43 years since I was wounded and my leg is still not right and it never will be. It aches more in the cold weather, I think the shrapnel must have damaged the nerves in my leg because I have constant muscle spasms which at times restricts the movement in my leg, I have grown so used to the spasms that sometimes I don't realise that it's happening. The Australian Army have me registered as 30% disabled, but when I see on TV our soldiers with horrific injuries, some that have been caused by land mines, it makes me realise just how fortunate I am.

Because I was a reinforcement in Vietnam I only served about 8 months, but the original soldiers from 6 RAR had completed 12 months. It was first thought that the reinforcement guys would have to stay on in Vietnam until they had also completed 12 months, or close to it. However, that didn't happen and we were allowed, thankfully, to leave with the rest of the Battalion. But I seem to recall at one point I was considering volunteering to stay on so that I could save some more money. But having given it some thought I changed my mind, because if anything would have happened to me during that time I would only have had myself to blame. I had been wounded once and I was still around to tell the tale, I didn't want to chance my luck again!

CHAPTER 21

FINAL DAY IN VIETNAM

Dear Mam

Thanks very much for your letter. I'm replying to it straight away because in the next few hours we'll be leaving Vietnam.

We've now left the Horseshoe camp and we're back in Nui Dat and preparing our gear ready to leave. We'll be flying out of here in helicopters and landing directly onto HMAS Sydney which a troop carrier. Then we'll be sailing to Brisbane, which should take about fourteen days. So Mam all your worries will then be over.

I'm sorry this is such a short letter Mam but I'm sure you'll forgive me under the circumstances.

I'll drop you a line as soon as I arrive back in Australia.

Look after yourself,

Your loving son
Derek xxxx

Memories...

Just before we were ready to leave Nui Dat, Alpha Company were addressed by the Commanding Officer. It was an emotional time for us all. A copy of his speech was given to every soldier of the Company. I kept mine and I still have it to this day.

COMMEMORATIVE SERVICE
A COMPANY 6 RAR 29 MAY 1967
ADDRESS BY COMMANDING OFFICER

On the last day of our tour of active service in Vietnam it is fitting that one of our final acts as a rifle company should be to worship together, and to remember our dead.

We should be thankful, humbly thankful, that the sacrifices of this Company have not been heavy. We mourn from our own ranks Private John Ashton, the only man of A Company who paid the greatest sacrifice of giving his life in the cause for which we fought.

Yet we have seen others die, and we have seen men noble in their courage and determined in the face of death. We are mindful of the men of other companies and of other battalions, who have died in this war. They have lost their lives in the service of their country, and we have done our best to ensure that their sacrifice was not in vain.

Our enemies, too, should be remembered. Our task was to fight them and kill them. And this we have done. But we must remember them as men, and even more, as soldiers fighting for a cause in which they believed.

Our joy at the prospect of returning home is tempered by the memory of our comrades who have fallen in battle, and who shall not be sailing with us. And to their loved ones, our homecoming can only be a painful reminder of the men they mourn.

Be it good luck or divine intervention, we know that others have suffered more than we, and that this Company, which fought in every major engagement, has endured much but suffered little. We must, for this, be humbly grateful.

As the bugler now plays the greatest salute that we as soldiers can give to others, let us pay tribute to those men who have fought well, who died bravely, and whom we shall always remember.

We left Nui Dat as planned and we all landed safely on HMAS Sydney, which was harboured in the bay of Vung Tau.

We used a shuttle service on Chinook helicopters until the whole battalion was onboard. For those of you who are not familiar with the Chinook helicopter, they are the long sausage shaped and have double rota blades, one at the front and one at the rear. Amazingly these choppers are still in use today in such places as Afghanistan and Iraq.

Once all of us were onboard it was only a matter of fourteen days sailing time to Australia and my tour of duty in Vietnam was over. When I finished my 2 years National Service, I was on reserve for the following 3 years, although I was never recalled for duty during that time.

My Army service had taken me to Vietnam, The Philippines and three states in Australia and for that I received the following 5 medals; The Vietnam Medal, The Vietnamese Campaign Medal, The Active Service Medal, The Defence Medal and the National Service Medal. As an Englishman I feel very proud to have been in the Australian Army and to have served with a great bunch of Aussies.

Australian Active Service Medal 1945-1975   Vietnam Medal   Australian Defence Medal   National Service Medal 1951-1972   Vietnamese Campaign Medal

CHAPTER 22

SAILING BACK TO AUSTRALIA

Dear Mam

I thought I'd drop you a line to let you know how things are going. We landed safe and sound onboard HMAS Sydney and we are now sailing towards Australia.

It really is a fantastic feeling being able to relax and to know you don't have to go on anymore patrols. The meals are great too, it makes a nice change from ration packs. We're due to arrive in Brisbane on the 14th June and I think the following day we march through the city centre. After that I'll be heading back down to Melbourne and I should get about 3 or 4 weeks leave.

Well Mam, I'm glad Vietnam is now in the past, but I don't regret ever being there. It's made me realise how lucky I am to have a home and family like mine. I appreciate that now more than I've ever done before.

I've bought two bottle of champagne, one pink and one white. I'll open them when I get to Melbourne and have a celebration drink.

In 4 months time I'll be on another ship but this time it will be sailing to England.

I'll finish off now Mam, so look after yourself.

Your loving son

Derek xxxx

Memories...

It took 14 days to sail from Vietnam to Australia. And during the voyage it was the first time in 8 months that I felt I could totally relax. We had hot meals every day and I think for about the first time in 8 months I left food on my plate because I was full up! Whatever weight I lost in Vietnam I think I put back on in that fortnight.

The only problem I had onboard was I found it difficult to sleep at night. I'm not sure why that was. Perhaps it has something to do with lying in a hammock for the first time. I always imagined hammocks would be really comfortable, but I found them just the opposite, especially when you tried to turn over. Being suspended and swaying to and fro with the motion of the ship made me want to get out and sleep on the top deck. However, there was no way I was going to say anything to anybody for fear of being laughed at, especially after some of the places we had slept in, in Vietnam.

As we approached Brisbane, we could see along the quayside family and friends who were out in force to welcome us home. It was a very emotional time as you can imagine. In Vietnam they were tough soldiers, but on home soil and seeing their loved ones for the first time in 12 months, it was only natural for them to let their defences down and shed a tear or two. There was nobody there to meet me, but I'm sure if there had of been I would have reacted in the same way. However, I wasn't the only one who had no family or friends to meet them.

Some of the guys lived as far away as Adelaide or Perth. I know it's not the other side of the world like England, but they were still thousands of miles away from Brisbane.

Once the reunion with family and friends was out of the way, it was time for the Battalion to march through the city centre of Brisbane. Hundreds of people had turned out to line the streets and as we passed through they all applauded. It was a very proud moment for all of us.

When the march-through was over everyone went their different ways with family and friends. Me and another soldier Ray Webb, who was from Perth in Western Australia, and like me had nobody to meet him, decided to find a pub a little bit off the beaten track so we could get some peace and quiet. We found a little pub in a side street and there was about half a dozen people inside and as we walked in they all stood up and applauded us. We went to the bar and ordered a couple of beers and as we went to pay the landlord said "These are on the house lads". It was a really great feeling to be appreciated like that.

During my time in Vietnam I'd managed to save $2000, which was a fair amount in those days. The Aussies were paid good money in Vietnam and we didn't have to pay tax either. I believe we were on even more money than the Yanks.

Anyway, when I left Brisbane I made my way back down to Melbourne to stay once again with my Aussie family. They were really pleased to see me, as I was to see them. I was expecting Don to be there too but he was still in Puckapunyal. Don didn't go to Vietnam, much to the relief of his family, he was such a good soldier that after his basic and corps training he became a full corporal, and he ended up training recruits. We met up at a later date and had quite a few drinks together. I also looked up my old mate Vic, who at the time was living in St Kilda. He had been involved in a bad car accident just before I went to Vietnam. He suffered a broken nose and a fractured leg, but he wrote to me saying that he was expecting a big compensation cheque. As it happened he had just received the payment when I met up with him. He got $2500, so between us we weren't short of a few bob, but looking back that could have been the problem.

We found out that my cousin Les was now working in Newcastle which was just north of Sydney, so we decided to go up there to see him.

We got a friend of ours who had an old banger to take us up there. The distance from Melbourne to Newcastle is about a thousand miles, so we wondered if it was wise to travel all that way by car, especially as the car didn't look very reliable. However, in the end we decided to give it a go and we were really glad we did because some of the scenery on the trip was fantastic.

When we got to Newcastle we met up with Les and it was the first time I'd seen him since I went into the Army 21 months earlier. Anyway, we spent the weekend with him and we had a great time and I think that convinced Les that he wanted to come back to Melbourne with us. He had a job in Newcastle but thought he wouldn't have a problem finding work in Melbourne. Me and Vic told him about the money we had and said that we would help him out until he got fixed up with a job. Vic didn't have a job either so we all headed back to Melbourne.

I still had 3 months left to serve in the Army so out of the three of us I was the only one earning some money. I was posted back to Puckapunyal, but the last 3 months that I spent there are a complete blank to me. When I came back from Vietnam all I seem to remember is being on leave, but I can't see how I could have had that much time off. I know that a lot of the soldiers have trouble adapting to life once they come back from a war zone, and looking back I think that I was no exception because I had a drink problem, which was probably the reason for my amnesia.

With all the money Vic had, he didn't bother to look for a job and Les never bothered either, even though he didn't have any money, me and Vic subsidised him.

Every morning at 10 o'clock the three of us used to stand outside the pub waiting for the doors to open and at the end of the night we would fall out of there. This continued day after day, week after week. In the past I had always had a good appetite but as the weeks and months went by I was eating less and drinking more. The pubs used to serve lunch, dinner and supper so you didn't even have to leave the pub to get something to eat. As time went by I started to skip lunch, then I would miss dinner and then maybe just have a burger for supper and that was it. Everybody knows that drinking on an empty stomach isn't good for you and I think at one point I think my weight dropped to below 9 stones. This drinking went on for a couple of months and eventually I thought to myself if this carries on none of us are going to have any money to get our fares home. So, the three of us agreed to book our tickets before that happened. Les still hadn't found a job and he didn't have any money so it was left to me and Vic to pay for his ticket, with Vic paying the bulk of it.

We booked our passage on an Italian ship "The Castel Felice", it was due to leave Melbourne at the end of October 1967. We bought the cheapest tickets available at a cost of $300 each that is about £140. When I was discharged from the Army on 28th September, I picked up the last of my wages that was practically all the money that I had. The $2000 I had saved up in Vietnam was gone and Vic was down to the last few dollars of his $2500, and Les, well he never had any money in the first place.

Our sailing date was just over three weeks away so we all agreed to find a job so we could have some money for the five and a half week journey home.

I managed to get a job working as a conductor on the Melbourne trams. I don't think the pay was fantastic but at least I was earning some money. However, Vic and Les never even bothered looking for work, they just continued to get pissed every day with the last of the money. I was absolutely furious, so I confronted them and asked them what was going on. I asked them, how the hell are we going to manage on the ship for all that time without any money, but it made no difference, my words fell on deaf ears. I really lost my temper with them and it very nearly came to blows.

Anyway, I continued working up to the sail date and they still didn't bother looking for work. It was just as well that our tickets included all meals otherwise we would have starved on the journey home. So, with both Vic and Les now skint and me with about $100, the prospect of a pleasant journey home seemed remote to say the least. However, my first priority was to say goodbye to my adopted Aussie family, who over the years had welcomed me into their home, and even during the difficult times when I was drinking heavily, they always looked after me. But their kindness was never ending because when I said goodbye to them they gave me a beautiful Seiko wristwatch as a going away present.

Once we boarded our ship we went straight to our cabin, which was down a flight of stairs, then another and another.... I was beginning to think that our cabin was in the engine room! But I suppose that's what you get when you buy the cheapest tickets, however we still managed to have a bloody good laugh about it.

CHAPTER 23

THE VOYAGE HOME

In late October 1967 we set sail from Melbourne and headed up the coast of Australia to our first port of call, which was Sydney. We were allowed to go ashore when we got there because we had to pick up more passengers and we would be in port for about 3 hours. The three of us decided to go into the city for a few drinks and we headed to the nearest pub. After a while a young girl aged about 18 years came over to us and started chatting. We all had quite a lot to drink and it became obvious that she was touting for business. We told her that between us we had very little money and besides that we had a ship to catch in less than an hour. However, that didn't seem to put her off because she said she would come back to our cabin and offered her services for free. So we headed off back to the ship with her and Vic took her to our cabin. When the ship was ready to leave the siren sounded for all visitors to go ashore, but she was still in the cabin with Vic. Me and Les burst into the cabin and told her to get out because the ship was sailing, but she said she wanted to stay on until it got to New Zealand, which was our next port of call. I was convinced that she had planned this from the moment we met her in the pub. Anyway by now the ship had set sail which meant we were now harbouring a stowaway in our cabin! The cabin was so small that it only had room for 2 bunk beds and a sink which made it impossible for her to hide anywhere. The other problem was that we were sharing our cabin with another guy who we'd never met before. He was travelling on his own and he was about our age. I can still see the look of amazement on his face when he first walked in and saw the girl lying in the bed. We explained to him how it all came about and he agreed not to say anything. But the next day one of the stewards discovered her, he approached us and said he would have to report it to the Captain unless we gave him some money. All the money "we" had, had all gone, but even if we had some money I wouldn't have given him any. So, it wasn't long afterwards that we were taken to the Captain's office and we were given a real dressing down and let off with a caution. The girl was locked up in the hold and we never saw her again. I apologised to the guy from our cabin for getting him dragged into it.

So you could say it wasn't the best of starts to our voyage home. We were all skint having spent the last of our money in the boozer and we still had a 5 week journey ahead of us, and after just a couple of days on board we were already in trouble with the Captain, I thought to myself what else could go wrong?. I didn't have to wait long to find out, except this time it was only me that was affected.

We had just left New Zealand and when I woke up in the morning I felt a pain in the back of my neck. At first I didn't take much notice of it, I thought that maybe it was just the way I had been sleeping. But after a few days the pain began to get worse, and then a large swelling appeared on the back of my neck, it was red and inflamed. I just thought it was the start of a boil or abscess and that I would let it come to a head. However, the following day the pain was worse and the swelling was beginning to push my head downwards. Eventually I went to see the ship's Doctor who diagnosed a cyst. He said that I needed surgery to remove it as soon as possible because it was infected and the infection was spreading.

As it was an Italian ship as you would expect all the crew were also Italian, including the Doctor. As I recall his English wasn't very good but I understood him when he said he wanted money before he would perform the operation. I can't remember how much he wanted, but whatever it was, I didn't have it. We had a bit of a discussion and in the end he reluctantly agreed to operate free of charge. The following day I was on the operating table and for some reason I was expecting a general anaesthetic, but to my surprise he only gave me a local one. The doctor injected a needle into my neck, waited a couple of minutes, and then he cut me with a scalpel. Immediately I jumped up and shouted out, I thought is this my low pain threshold playing me up again! However he quickly apologised to me and said "I'll have to inject you with another needle", but I think he hadn't given it enough time for the anaesthetic to take effect, or perhaps he was saying to himself "I'll make this little bugger suffer some pain for not paying me!" My ordeal wasn't over yet, because after he had removed the cyst, as suspected a number of channels leading from it had become infected. The doctor explained to me that he would have to use electricity to stop the infection from spreading any further! I thought is he having a laugh? First he cuts me without anaesthetic and now he wants to electrocute me! He told me to place my hand on what looked like a metal plate which had a wire leading from it. He then proceeded to give me electric shocks to the infected areas at the back of my neck. I think there were about a dozen altogether and with each shock I couldn't help but shout out loud. When it was finally all over I came out of the surgery with a bandage that went around my neck and up and around the top of my forehead. I looked like I'd just come out of a war zone. When the bandages came off and the stitches were taken out I was left with a scar that was shaped liked a piece from a jigsaw puzzle. But I was just glad that it was all over.

As we continued our voyage we headed out into the Pacific Ocean. As we approached the island of Tahiti one of the crew had put up a notice asking if any passengers would like to put their names down to play a football match against the crew. It also said that there would be free transport to the venue and there would be free drinks. Me, Les and Vic decided that seeing as everything was free we would put our names forward and give it a go. We also thought that if we won the match their might be a prize. When we got to the venue I was quite surprised to see that there was a good turn out from the locals who had come to watch the match. When the passengers team got changed at the side of the pitch we looked more like a rag-bag Army than a football team. Some of us wore vests and trainers, some wore shoes, and some even had on long trousers, but just the same we were all keen to give it our best shot, that is, until we saw the opposition coming out of the changing room. Every one of their players was immaculately turned out. They were all in matching kit and looked like they were a professional football team and if I hadn't of known any better would have sworn we were playing A.C.Milan. Any thoughts of us winning the game soon disappeared and as you can guess we were completely annihilated as the score line reflected at the end of the game.... 23 - 0.

When we arrived at the Panama Canal we were allowed to get off the ship to do some sightseeing in Balboa. But as it turns out we didn't get the best of receptions from the locals. Apparently, Vic, Les and me ended up in a part of the town that was a no-go area for tourists. As we walked along one of the streets it was like a shanty town and we sensed that something was wrong. We were the only white guys and people started coming out of their homes and shouting abuse at us. We didn't know what they were saying but it was clear by the anger on their faces that it wasn't anything pleasant. We did a quick about turn and as we did they started throwing stones at us. In the end we had to leg it to the ship as fast as we could.

Back on board ship we told one of the crew what had happened and he said that they probably thought that we were wealthy American tourists! We had a good laugh over that because if they had known that we were three English guys who were absolutely skint they might have invited us in for a cup of tea!

During the voyage we got to know some of our fellow passengers really well and when they found out about our predicament of having no money they often bought us drinks and gave us cigarettes. A family from Manchester and a couple of Aussie guys spring to mind. However, one person in particular I will never forget, because his generosity to us was overwhelming. His name is Barry Fairclough and he is a fellow Scouser. Over the five week journey he bought us drink, after drink, after drink and never once said he wanted repaying. I'll be forever in his debt. Thanks to him and all the other generous people our journey was made a lot more enjoyable. I used to bump into Barry from time to time when I worked on the buses, and we would always have a chat about Australia and the time we spent together on that voyage home.

At the end of the voyage we disembarked in Southampton and everyone said their goodbyes. We still didn't have any money to get home but Les had sent his Dad a telegraph message asking for some money. His Dad sent it to a Post Office in Southampton and we were then able to buy train tickets and be on our way to Liverpool. Once on board the train we had a 5 hour journey ahead of us. I must have got in touch with my family when I got to Southampton because when we got into Lime Street station in Liverpool waiting for me when I got off the train was my brother Brian. We gave each other a big hug. It was great to see him again after nearly 3 years and in all that time he didn't look any different, except for what he was wearing! He had a full length fur coat on, I remember saying to him "does my Mother know you're wearing her coat!" and he laughed. It also made me realise that I was back into the cold weather again. As we were about to walk to the car Brian said that we would have to hang on for a few minutes, it turned out that he had phoned the Liverpool Echo and they were sending a reporter to interview me about my experiences in Vietnam. All I wanted to do was to go home and see my Mam and Dad, so when the reporter turned up we made arrangements to do the interview at another time. A few weeks later an article about me appeared in the Liverpool Echo.

When we pulled up outside my home my Mother was waiting for us at the front door. I got out of the car and she ran down the path and threw her arms around me and tears of joy ran down her face. I managed to hold back the tears, but it was very emotional, as we continued to hug one another. When we went inside the house I hugged my Dad and we all sat up talking into the early hours of the morning. I confessed to them that I felt ashamed after nearly 3 years away from home I had returned without a penny to my name. But my Mother assured me that all her prayers had been answered when I returned home safe and in one piece. I thought that was the nicest thing she could have said to me and it helped me to feel a lot better.

Mr. Ponting

Back from Vietnam—a Liverpool railwayman

A young Liverpool railwayman has just returned home after serving for a year with the Australian forces in Vietnam. And he is still convinced that his call-up was a mistake in the first place.

Mr. Derek Ponting, of 215 Lower House Lane, Fazakerley, emigrated to Australia in February, 1965, and was working as a trainee shunter in Melbourne when the call-up papers arrive.

"I think you really have to be in Australia at least two years before you're liable for National Service," he said.

"But I didn't say anything about it. I didn't mind—not even going to Vietnam."

Leg wound

He was posted there for a year—the usual Australian tour of duty in Vietnam —in October, 1966. Two months later he received a leg wound from a Vietcong booby trap and spent four weeks in an American army hospital.

After that he returned to the front, and stayed in Vietnam until three months ago. Then he took a holiday in Australia before coming back home.

As an infantryman Mr. Ponting found conditions pretty tough.

"The terrain varies. Apart from the jungle, there are the rubber plantations. It was all rubber plantations near the main Australian camp, and that's easy to move about in. Then there are the rice fields, and the bamboo. The bamboo's the worst."

May go back

But he came to like the South Vietnamese themselves.

Despite his possibly accidental army service with the Australians, and the fact that he is still on reserve to the Australian army for the next three years, Mr. Ponting is thinking of going back there.

"One reason I didn't mind going in the army was that I could save money in Vietnam which I couldn't in Australia. I was able to save enough to come home and see my family."

CHAPTER 24

ADJUSTING TO LIFE AT HOME

Although I was over the moon seeing my mother, father and brother for the first time in nearly three years, it wasn't long before I started to miss Australia. I became very depressed over the following weeks and I couldn't really put my finger on what was really causing it. I didn't have a job which didn't help matters and I had to depend on my parents for money if I wanted to go out for a drink. That was also a problem. I couldn't get used to the English beer, which was made from hops and was always served warm! The Aussie beer was always served ice cold. The nearest thing I could get to an Aussie beer was draught double diamond, but it didn't taste anywhere near as nice and it was never cold enough. I'd be sitting in the pub with my brother and mates but I wasn't really enjoying myself. I would find my thoughts drifting back to Australia and Vietnam. I used to go to the toilet and instead of coming back to join the guys I would just leave without a word to anyone and walk the couple of miles home. This happened on a number of occasions. When I stayed in at home I used to pace up and down in the living room and that was causing a different kind of worry to my Mother, than it did when I was in Vietnam. I can't really recall everything that was going through my mind at the time however, it's now common knowledge that some soldiers returning from a war zone suffer with post traumatic stress disorder. I'm not saying that was the cause of my problems, but there was something that just wasn't right with me. Perhaps it was a combination of not having a job, no money, the beer and missing the camaraderie of my Army mates I don't really know, but it was so much out of character for me to act like that.

Anyway, after about a month or so I managed to get a job as a van driver, delivering motor parts to garages throughout the north west. It was the first time I had money of my own and I no longer had to depend on my parents for handouts. As the time went by I changed jobs a couple of times and then managed to get a decent job as a Bus Driver. I used to drive double decker buses that we called back loaders, because the passengers boarded at the rear, the same type that Reg Varney used to drive in the hit T.V. series "On the Buses". I liked the job because I was in the cab on my own and I was sort of my own boss and I started to see life in a better light.

I had a couple of on-off romances and it wasn't long before that I married a girl called Irene, after going out with her for about a year. However, the marriage didn't last and we were divorced not long after. I think that I was probably more to blame than she was. Anyway, life carries on and soon after that I met Pat.

I knew Pat from a previous meeting in the local pub and I fancied her then. We started going out together and eventually married in December 1979 and our daughter Debbie was born the following year. I had a steady job and the pubs had now started to sell cold draught lager, Aussie style, so things were definitely looking up at last.

In 1991, me and Pat had been married for twelve years and in all that time Pat had heard all my stories about Vietnam and all about the friends I had made in Australia, and of course my Aussie family too. One day when I came home from work Pat said there was a letter for me. When I opened it I couldn't believe my eyes when I saw what was inside. Without me knowing, Pat had bought me a ticket to Australia. No, it wasn't a one way ticket either, although I couldn't have blamed her if it was, considering all the stories I had bored her with over the years. It was a return ticket to Melbourne and I was absolutely thrilled. So in November 1991, I prepared for my first visit to Oz in 24 years.

CHAPTER 25

RETURN TO OZ – 1991

So once again I was off on my own flying to Melbourne, Australia, only this time it wasn't going to take as long as before to get there, and with less touchdowns. My first stop was in the middle east and the second stop in Darwin and then onto Melbourne.

I wondered what changes had gone on over the past 24 years and I suppose one of the first things I noticed that was different was the amount of Asian looking people who were walking around and also driving the taxis and trams. I think they were mainly Chinese and Vietnamese.

I knew through correspondence that the Cass family were no longer living in the same house where they had made me welcome so many years ago. Mr and Mrs Cass were now staying in a retirement home and all their children Don, Val, Robert and Julie were married with children of their own. Fortunately, they all lived within close proximity of one another which made things easier for us all to arrange a get-together.

When we did meet up it was really fantastic. Don, Val, Mr and Mrs Cass looked really well and it didn't seem as though they had changed much at all. However, the twins Julie and Robert, who were only 12 years old when I left Australia, had obviously changed a lot. I wouldn't have recognised them if they hadn't have been with the rest of their family, but they looked great. They said that I hadn't changed much either, except that my once curly locks were fast disappearing. The following day I visited Don's home and also Val's.

I wasn't staying with any of the family this time. I was staying with Bryan, a mate from back home who had emigrated to Oz a few years earlier. I used to write to Bryan before I left and in one of his letters he told me he had met two guys who had told him that they were in the Army with me... what a small world! It turned out to be John Johnson and Alan MacMullen. Both of them were in 7 RAR with me and later in Vietnam. All three of us where British and ironically we were all called-up under the same circumstances having been in Australia for only about 6 months. John was a fellow Scouser and Macca was from Llandudno in Wales.

Anyway we all met us in a R.S.L. club and had a few drinks and a good catch up. At one point John surprised me when he asked me what type of pension I was getting from the Army. I told him I wasn't getting any pension. He said I should have been receiving one since 1967 because of the injuries I received to my leg. John was working on the welfare side of the Army as a volunteer and he had helped many soldiers who had been wounded, both physically and mentally, get pensions. For all his hard work and dedication to these ex-soldiers he was awarded by the Australian government with the OAM, (Order of Australia Medal) which is the equivalent of our OBE, I think. When I got back to England John sent me the forms to complete and eventually I was told that I was entitled to 30% disability pension and it was backdated for 3 months, which was the maximum time it could go back. So the previous 24 years that I could have been claiming had been wasted, however, without John's help and advice I wouldn't be getting anything at all, so thanks John! It seemed that no sooner had I arrived in Australia than it was time to return home, the 10 days that I spent there just flew over. But I was really pleased to see all the Cass family once again and sadly it was the last time that this would happen, because Don died of Cancer in 1999 and Mr Cass died in 2005. I miss them both and they will always be in my memory.

Robert, Me and Julie.
November 1991

Mrs Cass, Don, Me and Mr Cass.
November 1991

Back row: Val, Me, Mrs and Mr Cass.
Front row: Glen (Val's son)
Jim (Val's husband)
November 1991

Johno, Me and Macca. November 1991

Watersonia RSL Club Melbourne 1991.
Johno, Me, Parky and Macca. Three Scouses and a Welshman.
We all had one thing in common - we were all conscripted into the Australian
Army in 1965/66 and all served in Vietnam.

138

CHAPTER 26

VIETNAM VETS VISIT LIVERPOOL

Over the years four Vietnam veterans who had served with me have made visits to Liverpool. The first two to come over were John Johnson and Alan MacMullen. I met up with them at John's mother's birthday party in Netherton, and a good time was had by all.

Another Vietnam veteran who came over in 2003 was Graham Kelly and his wife Sue. They spent the weekend with us and we took them out and about and to our local social club.

The most recent visit was by Dave Hede and his wife Sue, they came in 2005 and they stayed in Liverpool for about 4 days and in that time I took them to the Beatles Museum at the Albert Dock and for a ferry ride across the Mersey. We also went to Anfield to watch Liverpool FC play Bolton Wanderers, and thankfully Liverpool won 1-0. Dave had been an LFC supporter ever since he had met me in Vietnam. After the match we finished the night off in our local social club. Dave and me talked about our times together in Vietnam and mentioned some of the other guys who had served with us. It was then that I got a shock when he told me that Johnny Needs had been killed by a landmine in 1969, during his second tour in Vietnam. Johnny was in Alpha Company with us on the first tour in 1966/67. I remember him as a very likeable bloke, so the news of his death really saddened me. Dave told me that a book had been published in Australia called "Long Tan and Beyond", by Lt Col Mollison. He said he would send me a copy of the book when he got back to Australia and true to his word a few weeks later I received the book. It was of particular interest to the likes of me and Dave because it was about Alpha company's involvement in 1966/67.

A large part of the book is taken up by the soldier's themselves giving their personal accounts of what happened. A number of letters appear in the book aswell, and one that caught my attention was from Johnny Needs sister Sue. In her letter she was encouraging the veterans to put pen to paper and tell some stories about the funny little things that happened in Vietnam, rather than the horrors of war all the time.

Well Sue, I've written this book and tried to tell my story as I remembered it and as you suggested I have included a little bit of humour along the way.

***

Me and Graham Kelly having a drink in our local social club.

Over the years I've often been asked if I'd ever consider returning to Vietnam as a tourist. I must admit it has crossed my mind a few times, but I have never really got round to it. If I did decide to go I'm sure it would bring back a lot of memories for me, even though I wouldn't expect it to look anything like it did in 1966/67. Only recently I found out from the 6 RAR "A" News website that two hotels had been built near to the site where the Aussies had their main camp in Vung Tau. However, the names of the hotels might put some people off! One is named "the Dic Star Hotel" and the other one is called the "Phuoc Dat Hotel" enough said!!

Me and Dave Hede at the Albert Dock in Liverpool.

A clipping from the Liverpool Echo of me and Davies reunion.

A HAPPY BLAST FROM THE PAST

Duo reunited after 38 years

By RUSSELL MYERS

A LIVERPOOL soldier had an emotional reunion with a Vietnam war comrade – 38 years after nearly blowing him up.

Derek Ponting, from Childwall, left Merseyside for Australia in 1965.

Less than two months later, at the age of 20, he was conscripted to Vietnam for two years of national service.

Derek was leading his Australian troop through dense jungle when he accidentally triggered a tripwire connected to a grenade.

It was then that an unusual friendship was formed with Aussie soldier and Liverpool FC fan David Hede.

Derek said: "I managed to do more damage to the Australian army than the Vietcong that day."

In the process of using the internet to track down former colleagues,

OLD DAYS: Derek and David as they were in Vietnam

Derek discovered one still has a piece of shrapnel embedded in his chest.

But he also discovered his old mate David and the duo decided to meet up.

He said: "I wanted to find out how the guys who were injured with me were getting on after all this time.

"I posted messages up on the internet and before long David replied.

"It's just great to see an old friend again after all this time."

David, from Brisbane, said: "It's great to meet up with Derek and to be shown around Liverpool.

"It was such a culture shock being back home for the first couple of years. I used to sleep on the floor for the first six months after coming back from the jungle."

The two served together for more than a year, before going their separate ways in 1967. They plan to meet again at a battalion reunion in 2010.

Derek said: "I can't wait to go back and catch up with some of the old crew.

"I'm sure it will be a momentous and emotional occasion."

- THE Vietnam war ran from 1962 to 1972.
- Australia became involved in the war via the SEATO agreement (South East Asian Treaty Organisation), created to oppose further Communist gains in Southeast Asia.
- 50,000 Australians saw service – 500 were killed.

BACK TOGETHER: Former army colleagues and friends Derek Ponting and David Hede   Picture: TONY KENWRIGHT

CHAPTER 27

THE 6 RAR REUNION

When Dave Hede visited me in March 2005, he told me that in June he would be attending the 40th Anniversary reunion of 6 RAR. The reunions are held every 5 years in Brisbane, where Dave lives, and I think that he has attended most of them. I had never been to any of them and I always hoped that one day I would be able to go. With Dave telling me all about the great camaraderie that still exists I was determined to attend the 45th Anniversary in June 2010. By that time I would be 65 years old in March, and also retired from the buses.

Fast forward 5 years and after working on the buses for 40 years I was finally retired. Anyway as I promised myself I was going back to Australia and for the first time I was going to attend a 6 RAR reunion. It would also be the first time that I wouldn't be going to Australia on my own, my wife Pat would be coming with me.

So we set off to Australia on 25th May 2010. We had decided to spend some time in Melbourne before going to the reunion in Brisbane. Mrs Cass, Val and her husband Jim were now living in Brisbane. Sadly, Mr Cass and Don were no longer with us so now there was only Robert, Julie and their families living in Melbourne. We made arrangements to meet up with them, and it ended up with Robert, Julie, her daughter Kim, Don's wife Joanne and her daughter Mandi all getting together. We had a really good time and a lovely meal and spent the evening catching up and chatting away. At the end of the night Joanne's daughter Mandi gave me a framed photograph of her Dad (Don) in his Army uniform. It now stands in a cabinet at home with the rest of my Army memorabilia.

Next on the agenda was to make contact with John Johnson, his wife Anita and Macca. I had met John and Macca the last time I visited Australia in 1991 and I also met them in Liverpool a couple of years after that. So, here we were once again. Joining us that night was another Army mate Mick. We got together at the RSL club in East Killor, Melbourne. Me and Pat had a wonderful night at the RSL, John had told them at the club that we had come over from Liverpool and that I had been in the Army with him in Vietnam. Much to our surprise they announced this over the microphone at the club and everyone stood up and applauded. We were given a lovely friendly welcome.

There were two other close friends I also had to get in touch with, and that was Kevin and Lloyd. The two of them had kept in touch with each other since they left the Army.

Although I'd spoken to both of them on the phone over the years, I hadn't seen them since the three of us had a brief meeting in Vietnam in 1967. So when I arrived in Melbourne I phoned Kevin first and his wife answered the phone and said "is that you Scouse"? "Yes", I replied, "sorry she said I've got some bad news for you, Kevin is in hospital, he suffered a heart attack a couple of days ago". She said that she hoped he would be home later that day. The problem was that he lived a couple of hundred miles away from where we were staying in Melbourne and I don't think he would have liked me to see him when he wasn't in the best of health and also he wasn't up to having visitors and the risks of getting too excited. So reluctantly we weren't able to go and visit him. However, I did speak to him on the phone on a number of occasions and we talked about the good times we used to have. Afterwards I phoned Lloyd and told him what had happened to Kevin. Initially the three of us were supposed to meet up, but now due to Kevin's predicament that was no longer practical. However, Lloyd was still determined to meet up with me even though he was looking after his elderly mother and he lived a few hours outside Melbourne. He said he would come into Melbourne by train, so we made arrangements to meet in Young and Jackson's pub opposite Flinders Street station. The first thing that crossed my mind was would we recognise each other after 43 years. Well when he first walked into the pub the answer was no, but after we eyed each other for a minute or two we did, and we laughed and hugged each other. It was 11.45 am and me, Lloyd and Pat chatted away for the next 7 hours! We reminisced about times gone by which brought loads of laughter and even the odd tear. Lloyd had brought with him a bag that was filled with old photographs. Lloyd's Dad had given him a camera when he went to Vietnam and he had taken hundreds of photographs and slides. At one point during the afternoon when we were looking at some old photographs an old man came over to us and said "excuse me, I don't mean to intrude but I couldn't help noticing the joy on your faces and I was wondering what the occasion is"? when I told him it was the first time that we had met since we were in Vietnam in 1967 he said "Oh well, that explains everything". Although there was only the three of us I've never known 7 hours go by so quickly in all my life. I walked Lloyd back to the station as I wanted to make sure he was okay after all the beer we had drunk. I said "let's hope it's not as long 'til we meet up again" and he said "Yeh, see ya buddy". So after spending a wonderful six days with friends in Melbourne our next destination was Brisbane.

When we arrived in Brisbane we were really pleased with our apartment. We were staying in Kangaroo Point and our apartment was on the eleventh floor, with spectacular views over the Brisbane River and along to the Storey Bridge. Probably it's not as famous as the Sydney Harbour Bridge but at night when it's light up it looks just as impressive.

If you wanted to travel into Brisbane city centre all we had to do was walk to the jetty that was just at the back of our apartments and jump on board the ferry and we were in the city centre in 10 minutes. The reunion was being held over three days. The first night on Friday was a meet and greet, the second night on Saturday was the Gala Dinner and on Sunday it was the memorial service followed by a barbecue.

Dave and Sue Hede picked us up on the first night and Dave had gone to the trouble of putting together a "before and after" photo album of some of the guys so that I would recognise them! However, I think I would have recognised them anyway. The night at the Bronco's club in Brisbane went really well and everyone made me and Pat really welcome. We all swapped stories about some of the things we got up to in Vietnam. It was a case of "do you remember this" and "do you remember that" One guy came over to me and said "Hey Scouse, do you remember the time you fell asleep when you were walking through the jungle". I wasn't exactly sure what he meant, but I think he was talking about the time that I've mentioned previously in the book when I was tail-end Charlie and I fell asleep because I was absolutely knackered. There were lots of stories that night that brought back loads of memories.

The following night Val and Jim joined us for the Gala Dinner. It was held at the Brisbane Convention Centre. The room was set out with different coloured balloons on large round tables, the colours represented different Company's and it was so well organised as you might expect from the Army. The colour for A Company was yellow and we made our way to our table with Val, Jim, Dave and Sue.

Once we had settled in the speaker welcomed us all and thanked us for supporting the occasion. He thanked all those people who had come all the way from Victoria and as far away as Western Australia. When he said that I looked at Pat and smiled as if to say what about us then? But, just then he said "would you please put your hands together for Derek and Pat Ponting for travelling all the way from the UK to attend here tonight". He asked them to stand up and we were warmly applauded. I must admit that I thought that it was a wonderful gesture. After that we had an excellent meal and the rest of the night went really well, with lots of dancing and laughter.

The last day of the reunion was held on Sunday at Enoggera Army camp. There was a memorial service to remember our fallen Army colleagues, which was very emotional for all of us. The Padre gave an emotional address. At the end of the service we were invited to place a poppy in the garden of remembrance. In the garden there were crosses with the names of the soldiers from the battalion who had lost their lives in Vietnam. I walked along and eventually stopped at the cross of John Ashton, were I placed my poppy.

To finish off the reunion we had a typical Aussie Barbie, fabulous roasted meats and lots and lots of ice cold beer, all served up by the present day squaddies. When it was over and we said our goodbyes I don't think that many of us were sober!

Me and Pat, Dave and Sue and some of the other guys and their wives headed back into Brisbane and later on we went for a meal...... to a Vietnamese restaurant!

So after 3 fantastic days the reunion came to an end and both me and Pat agreed that it was well worth the 12000 mile trip for that alone. It was now time to make arrangements to see my Aussie mum, Mrs Cass. She lived about 100 miles from Brisbane in a place called Elanora, which was up towards the Gold Coast. Although she was in her late 80s when I saw her she looked fantastic. After we hugged she took me and Pat to see her apartment which was in a small complex and was fully staffed with everything that she could need and she seemed very happy there. Later that day Val, Jim, Mrs Cass me and Pat went to the local RSL club and had a lovely meal and played the pokies (slot machines).

So the next day was to be the last of our holiday. Our stay in Brisbane was made that much better because Dave and Sue Hede took us out and about and showed us the sights of Brisbane. They also invited us to their home on the outskirts of the city. The gardens in their home backed onto a nature reserve that was full of wildlife. Sue showed us some recent photographs of a koala bear that had been sitting in a tree just a few yards away. We also saw parrots with the most spectacular colours.

Without the hospitality of Dave and Sue Hede our holiday would not have been as enjoyable, so a big thank you to them.

The next reunion will be in June 2015 and it will be to celebrate the 50th Anniversary of 6 RAR. I will be 70 years old when it takes place and me and Pat, god willing, will be there.

Reunited after 43 years. Army pal Lloyd and me reminiscing over an old photo.

Mrs Cass (my Aussie mum) and me together again.

Photos from the 45th 6 RAR Reunion.
6th, 7th and 8th June 2010.

Me, Pat, Jim and Val at the Gala dinner.

Me, Lt Col Charles Mollison and Pat.

Me and Pat relaxing after the memorial service at Enoggera Army Camp.
QLD

Me and other Vietnam Vets on Memorial Day.

Me (kneeling right) with "A" Company guys at the Gala dinner.

Guys from "A" Company 6 RAR.
Me, Besty, Rusty, Nigel, Dave and wives in a (you've guessed it)
a Vietnamese restaurant in Brisbane

POSTSCRIPT

Well, that's my story more or less brought up to date and taking everything into account I have been very fortunate in my life.

During the Vietnam War I was lucky in as much as I didn't see a lot of action. However, the dangers were always there every day.

The 500 Australians who lost their lives and the thousands injured both physically and mentally, some of whom I knew means that I will never forget my experience. Although I wasn't an Australian citizen my call-up was not an isolated case. Many more British subjects were also conscripted under the same circumstances as me, and I would imagine that they too would have a story to tell.

Everything that I have written in this book is a truthful account of events that happened as I remember them.

If, for any reason, there are any inaccuracies in my story, they are purely accidental, and I apologise for them, but most of the events did happen a long time ago now, so I hope I will be forgiven.

Derek Ponting

GLOSSARY

ARU - Australian Reinforcement Unit

ARVN - Army Republic of Vietnam

COY - Company

CSM - Company Sergeant Major

DMZ - Demilitarized Zone

MCG - Melbourne Cricket Ground

PTE - Private

NCO - Non-Commissioned Officer

R and C - Rest and Convalescence (Leave)

R and R - Rest and Recreation (Leave)

RSL Club - Returned Serviceman's Leave Club (Australia's equivalent to the British Legion)

SLR - Self Loading Rifle

WIA - Wounded in Action.

***

If you would to make any comments about the book, please fell free to contact me at: dearmam6@gmail.com